Made in Summerhill

Made in Summerhill

Humphrey A Truswell

Workshop Instructor at Summerhill School
Leiston, Suffolk, England

HAWTHORN BOOKS, INC.
Publishers/New York

MADE IN SUMMERHILL

Copyright © 1975 by Humphrey A. Truswell. Copyright under International and Pan-American Copyright Conventions. All rights reserved, including the right to reproduce this book or portions thereof in any form, except for the inclusion of brief quotations in a review. All inquiries should be addressed to Hawthorn Books, Inc., 260 Madison Avenue, New York, New York 10016. This book was manufactured in the United States of America and published simultaneously in Canada by Prentice-Hall of Canada, Limited, 1870 Birchmount Road, Scarborough, Ontario.

Library of Congress Catalog Card Number: 75-223

ISBN: 0-8015-7322-X

1 2 3 4 5 6 7 8 9 10

CONTENTS

INTRODUCTION *ix*

BOATS *3*
Paddle Boat *4*
Solid-Hull Boat *5*
Hollow-Hull Boat *6*
Section-Hull Boat *7*
Cabin Cruiser *8*
Fittings *9*
Tinplate Steamer *10*

GAMES *12*
Dominoes (Branding) *13*
Solitaire (Pegboard Game) *14*
Dice Game *15*
Jigsaw Puzzle *16*
Cube Game *17*
Cube Puzzle *18*
Ball Maze *19*
Pinball Machine *20*
Billiard Table *21*
Chess Set *22*
Whizzer *23*
Spinning Tops *23*
Construction Game *24*

GUNS *26*
Revolver *27*
Cut-Out Guns *28*
Tube Guns *29*
Extras *30*

AIR MACHINES *34*
Vintage Airplanes *35*
Propellers *36*
Basic Wind Machine or Windi *37*
Cycle Front-Forks Windi *38*

MIXED BAG *40*
Land Racer *41*
Thread-Spool Tanks *43*
Skate Board *44*
Whirlie Board *44*
Stilts *45*
Money Box *45*
Toilet-Roll Holder *46*
Tuck Box *47*
Letter Rack *48*
Mousetrap *48*
Picture Mounts *49*
Periscope *50*

Woodware 52	Dollhouse 80
Tin-Can Ware 53	Badges 82
Oil Lamps 54	Pipe Rack 82
Lampshades 55	Pencil Holder 82
Basic Cart 57	Cages 83
Tri Cart 58	Towel Racks 85
Model Cannons 60	Trays 86
Metal Cast 61	Birdhouses 87
Belts and Buckles 62	Solid Guitar Replica 89
Sandals and Flip-Flops 63	Wooden Spoon 90
Mobile 64	Plaster Eggs 91
Jewelry 65	Pull-Along Animal 92
Circular Stool 66	Chopping Board 93
Three-Legged Stool 67	Sundry Boxes 94
End-Frame Stool 67	Boot Pull 95
Laminates 68	Signs 96
Car Seats 70	Sundial 98
Bottle Cracking 72	Roll Blinds 99
Kite Reels and Kites 74	Clothespin Mat 100
Conker Snake 76	Glass Pictures 101
Name Tag 76	Trash Can Decoration 102
Robot 77	Storage Jar Decoration 103
Walkie-Talkie 77	Mirror Picture 104
Tin-Can Walkie-Talkie 77	**NOTES** 107
Wheels 78	

INTRODUCTION

ABOUT THE BOOK

At some point during the day I am inevitably asked "What shall I make?" My reply is likely to be "What do you want to make?" This in many ways is the essence of the Summerhill Workshop. Children can come in and either get on with making their latest idea or discuss some project or other with me. Some children simply like to flick through a book or magazine to get ideas and this is where *Made in Summerhill* will come into its own. It offers basic ideas or techniques that the child can then think about and use or adapt to his own purposes.

The aim is to stimulate a child to work out the idea creatively, not to give him or her a set of instructions to follow by rule. Gone forever, I hope, are the days when a whole class laboriously manufactured a teapot stand step-by-step. At Summerhill, children can work and progress at their own level and speed, without adults forcing their ideas, values, and standards upon them. I have deliberately left out detailed information about dimensions, etc. In my experience a mass of detail, while it may indeed be relevant, may not seem so to the child whose aim is to make a skate board or a machine gun—and may put him off altogether. When he needs for a specific reason, such as making a shelf to fit an alcove, to make a precise measurement, he will be willing to do it. However, until that situation arises it seems of little importance to him, or to me, whether a gun barrel is 2 inches long or 2¼ inches long; the child decides visually whether it is as he wants it.

Some of the ideas in the book were passing fads, like the stilts (see page 45). One child made a pair and in the course of five days the idea had caught on and some 24 pairs were made. The kids quickly mastered the idea of stilt walking and games such as stilt football evolved. This term, however, no one seems at all interested in stilts and so far no new craze has appeared. The workshop is producing its perennial stock of guns, badges, and tuck boxes. One summer term I set a fashion when I made what came to be called a windi. It consisted of a wooden propeller mounted in bearings, which I salvaged from various old cycles littered about the school, and a wind vane to keep the propeller facing into the wind (see pages 37–39). My reasons for making it were twofold. First, for the personal satisfaction I would get out of seeing it work in the wind, and second, to see how the community would react to it. The younger children took to the idea immediately and made smaller versions of the propeller to put on their airplanes, whilst the older ones seemed more inclined to throw rocks at it. However, after a term had elapsed they, too, began to show a more constructive interest in the idea, and Summerhill's breeziest spots were soon littered with windies of various shapes and sizes. In fact, at one point Ena's donkey, Cluney, was almost driven out of her paddock by the number that were attached to the trees there.

THE SUMMERHILL WORKSHOP

The workshop and artroom in Summerhill are not timetabled for individual classes, so that at any one time boys and girls of all ages from five to sixteen, can be found working together. In so doing, they influence each other. The influence is not all one way, that is, from the older to the younger children, but seems to find a norm between the two. Freedom, as opposed to license, is a large part of the Summerhill philosophy, and this is especially so in the workshop. Visitors often ask me about the safety aspect of the workshop, possibly imagining that children given a free hand with sharp tools will inflict damage on themselves and those about them. This isn't so. Children are sensible, and, so long as they don't interfere with anyone else, they are free to work as they see fit—although this doesn't mean that if I see a kid sawing laboriously I won't show him an easier way. I am very firm about safety with machinery and power tools. When someone needs to use a power tool he checks with me first, and it is understood that he is solely responsible for operating the machine until he is finished. I find that the simple act of asking me first makes the child more consciously careful.

Summerhill's workshop, affectionately referred to by one and all as "the woodwork shed," is equipped much as is any other workshop. However, because of the wide range of people using it we have work surfaces and benches at various heights. Equipment includes Neill's old belt-driven metal-turning lathe, which owing to its age and worn bearings, serves mainly to demonstrate basic lathe techniques. We also have a wood-turning lathe, probably the most dramatic piece of equipment—especially when someone is turning a bowl and streams of wood chips are flying off. This lathe doubles as a sander and is one of the most useful pieces of equipment that we have (see page 51). Children often have difficulty sawing a piece of timeber to a given line. The sander with its platform helps them true up their wood and is also very useful for shaping blocks of wood, making curves, etc. If someone slipped while on the sander it could cause a nasty burn, so I am continually reminding the children to be careful.

Making jewelry is a hobby of mine so I have a special evening class for it. Only children actually making jewelry are allowed in at this time, so we have the whole workshop space at our disposal. This arrangement also makes it easier to keep track of the special jewelry tools. The older girls show a good deal of interest in these classes. I don't see much of the girls during the day, when they are mainly concerned with academic lessons. Although their ideas often outstrip their technical ability, we usually manage to reach a compromise, and I am in fact constantly amazed at the standards they achieve.

I have mentioned materials that we use to make things. These of course are variable and you may wish to use others that are more readily available to you. Industrial offcuts are often a valuable source and one which I take advantage of whenever I can. The local engineering works lets us have at a very reasonable cost as much scrap metal as we can use. Lumberyards and manufacturing firms are usually willing to help out once they know that their waste can be put to good use in a school or by children. Scrapyards are a source of constant fascination to creative children, but you need to reach a strict understanding with the owner before you allow eager beavers to forage for valuable raw materials.

This then is a book of ideas that have evolved at Summerhill, some of them simple, some sophisticated. I hope that you will gain as much from it as I have from the children I work among, and that it will help you when as a parent or teacher you are asked "What can I make."

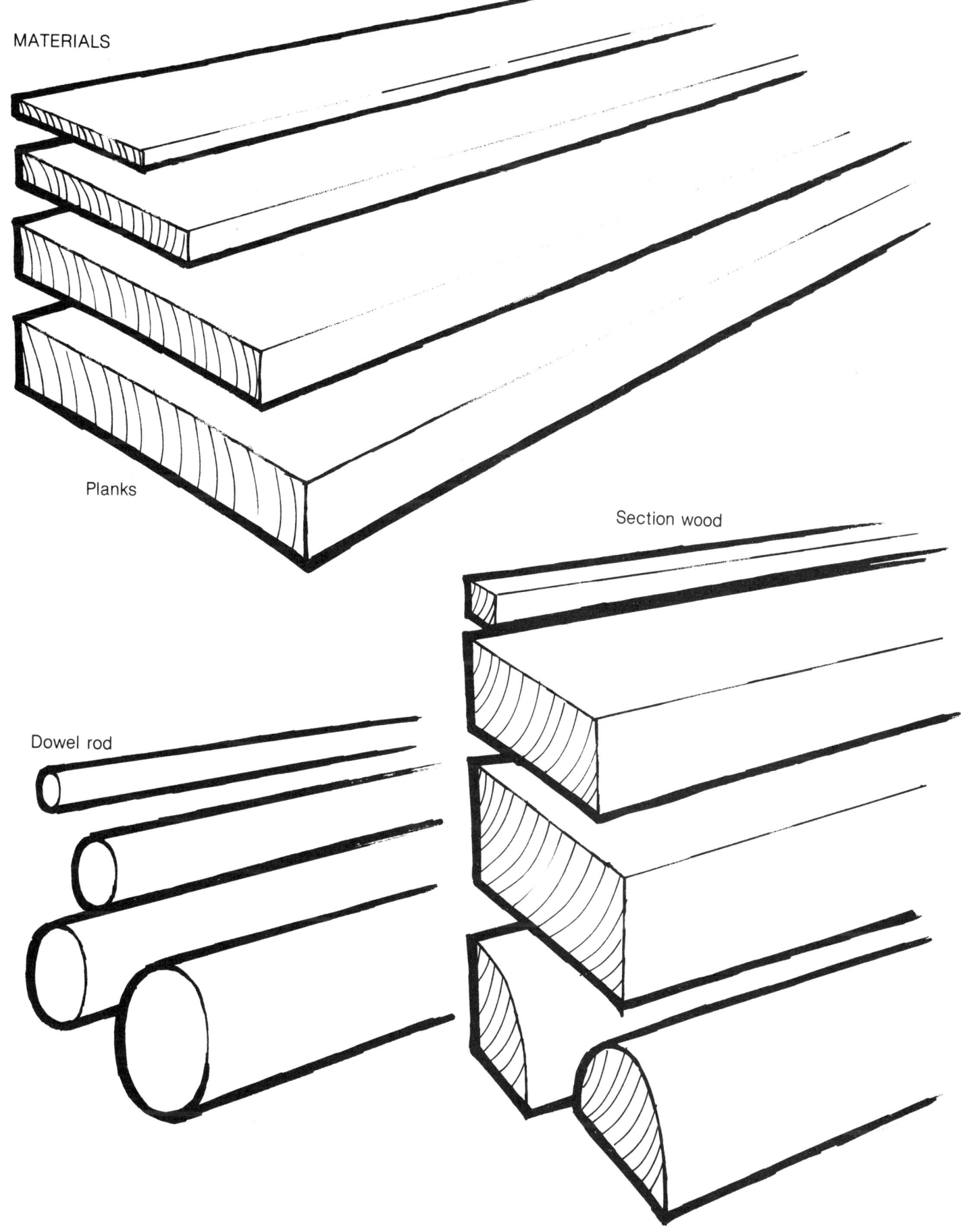

Made in Summerhill

BOATS

Things that float fascinate children; consequently boats of all shapes and sizes are made in the workshop.

Younger children tend to be satisfied with pieces of wood of any shape, so long as they float. Older kids want to get some realism into their work, so in this part of the book I have selected ideas for constructing various types of boats. If deep water is not at hand then the paddle boat will work in puddles, as will the steam boat. Otherwise, yachts and cruisers seem to be the most popular.

During the summer term when our swimming pool is in full use, this arouses enthusiasm for model boats, and we have periodic racing sessions to see whose theory on rigging and trim will prove most appropriate.

4
Paddle Boat

This paddle boat incorporates a twisted elastic band as its power source, and is good for one short, sharp burst.
    Materials: softwood plank, elastic band.

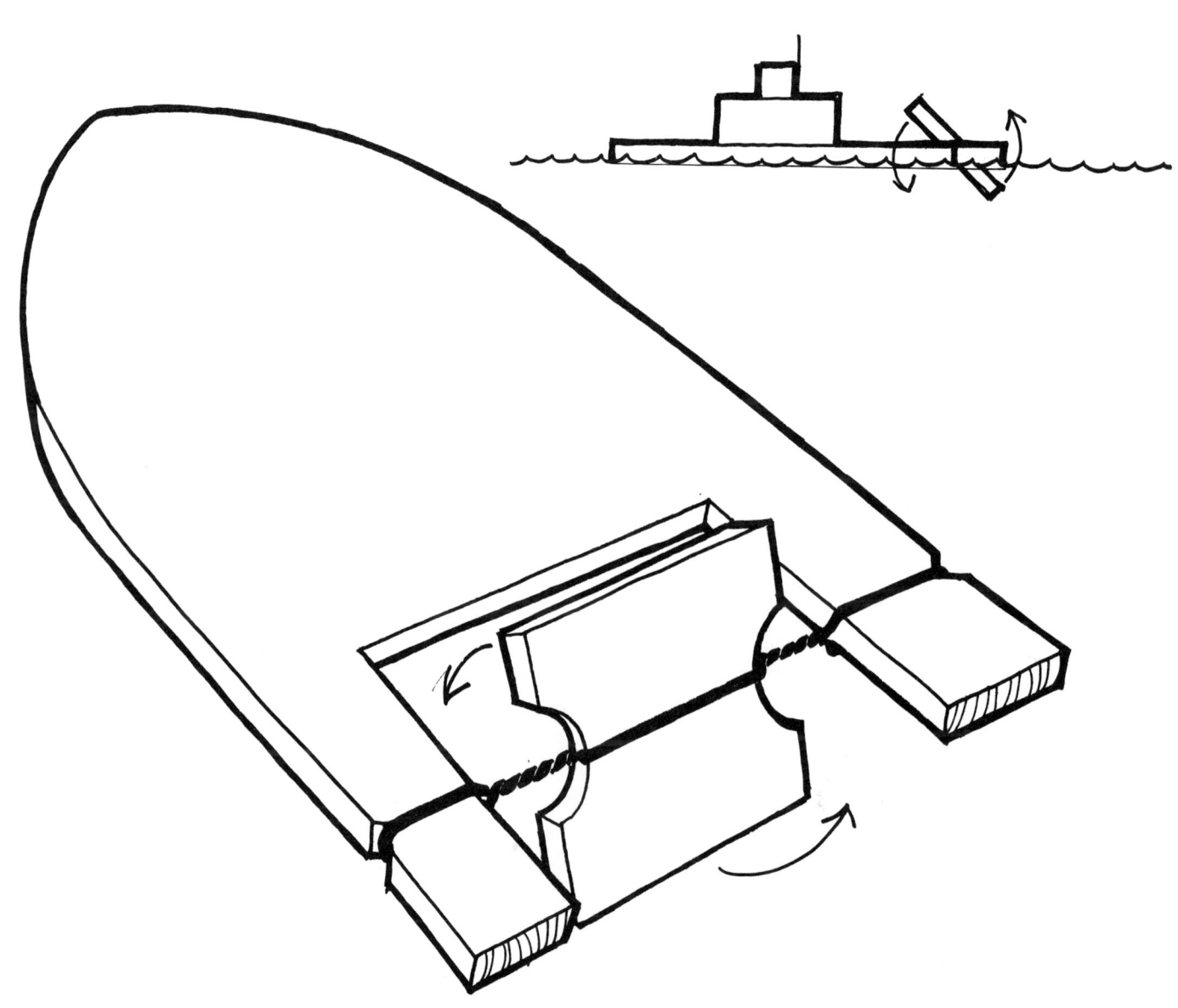

5
Solid-Hull Boat

Easy to shape and very stable due to side floats. Takes many of the problems due to trim and ballast out of sailing boats and is easily converted into a land yacht.

Materials: softwood section, dowel rod.

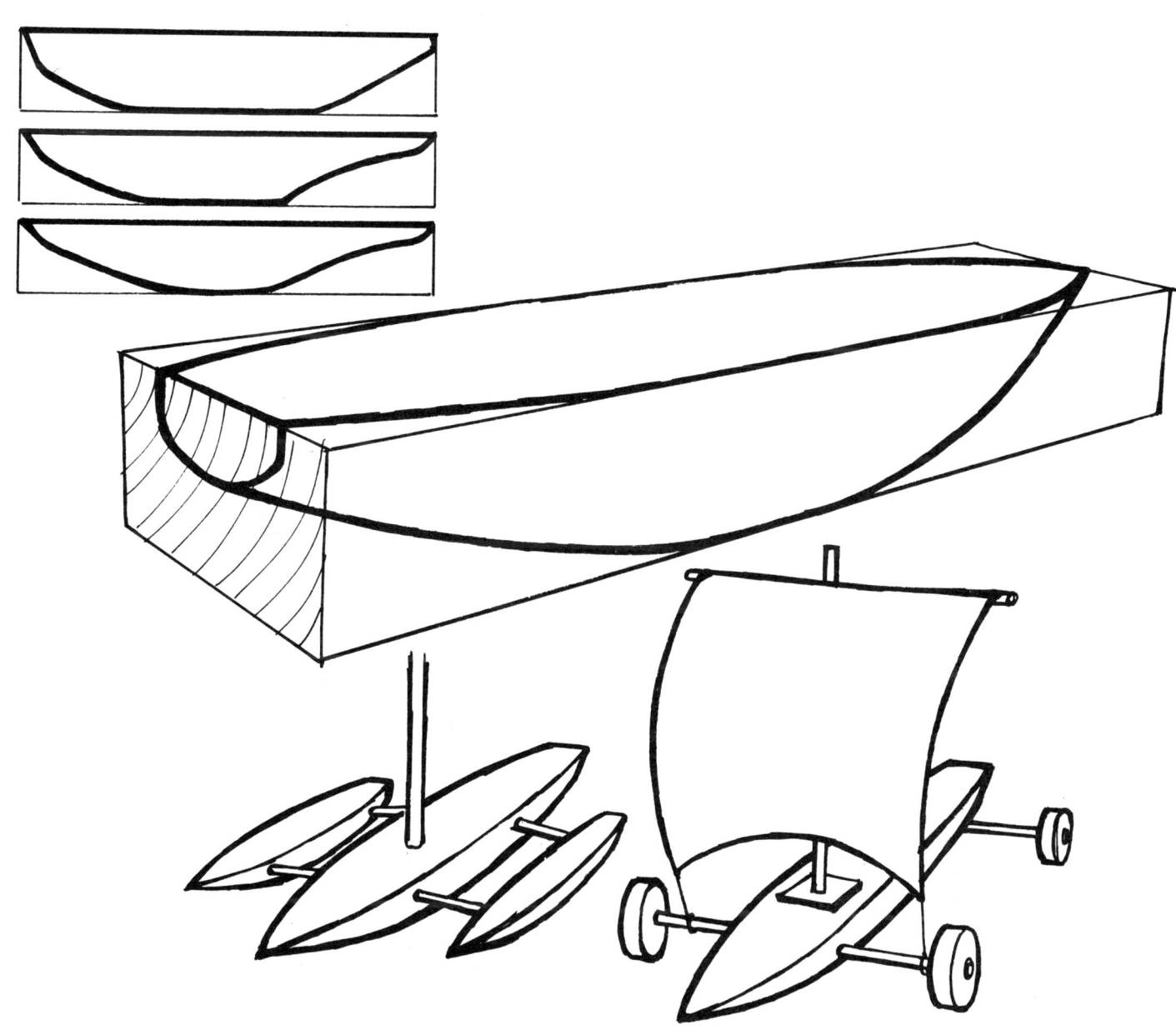

6
Hollow-Hull Boat

A lighter and consequently more buoyant boat may be made by hollowing out the hull (either by boring in or carving out) and covering the top. Rudders are easily made from a piece of metal rod with tinplate soldered on; same with keel.

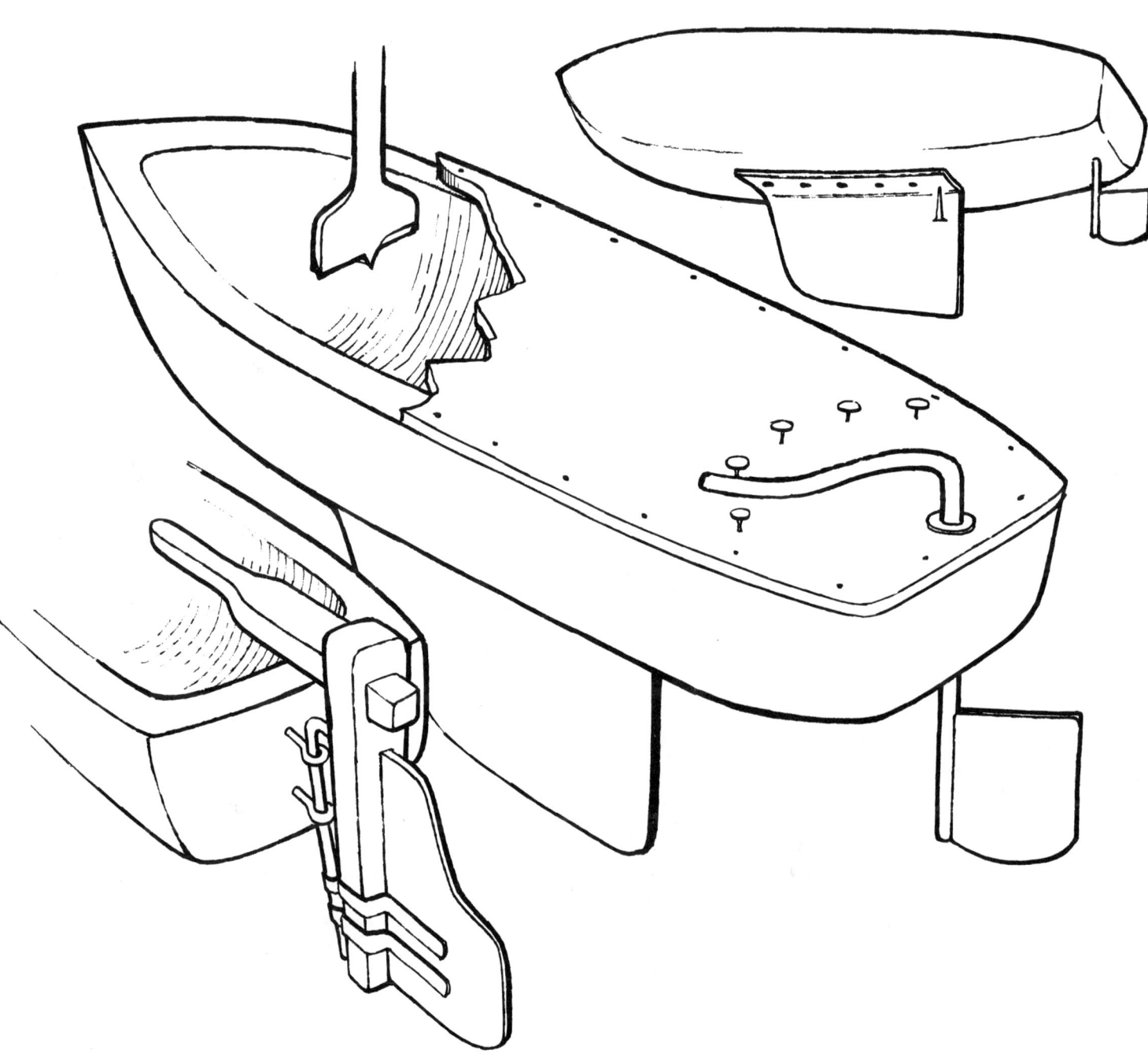

7
Section-Hull Boat

When a boat is made, say, 2 feet in length, this method of construction does away with the need for a long single piece of timber. The first boat like this made in the workshop used material from the scrap pile, but regular section timber is best to use.

Materials: sectioned softwood, waterproof glue.

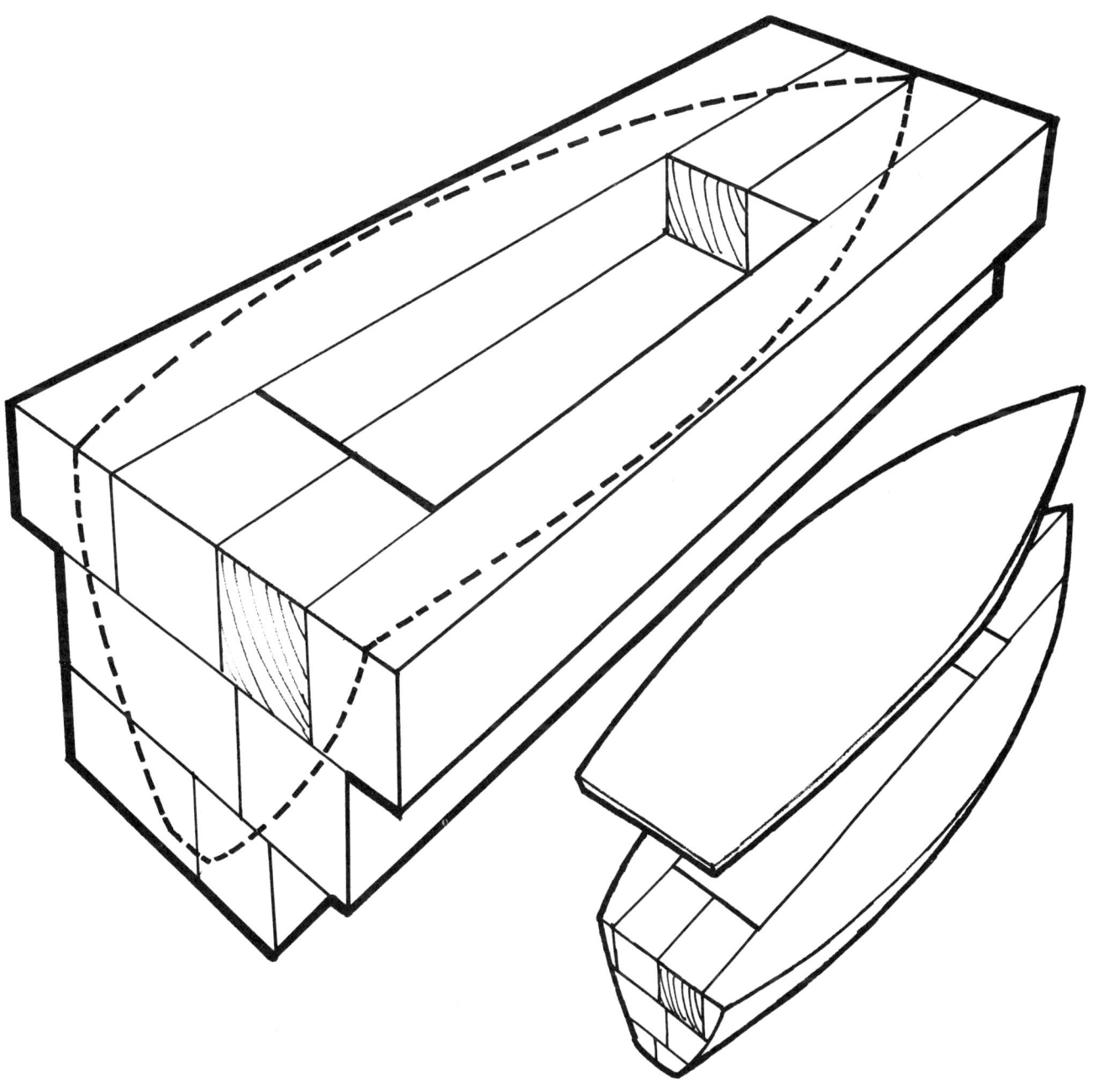

8
Cabin Cruiser

This type boat readily accommodates electric motors, batteries, etc., and still remains stable due to its flat bottom. Once the bottom is shaped the hull takes very little time to complete.

Materials: plywood, hardboard.

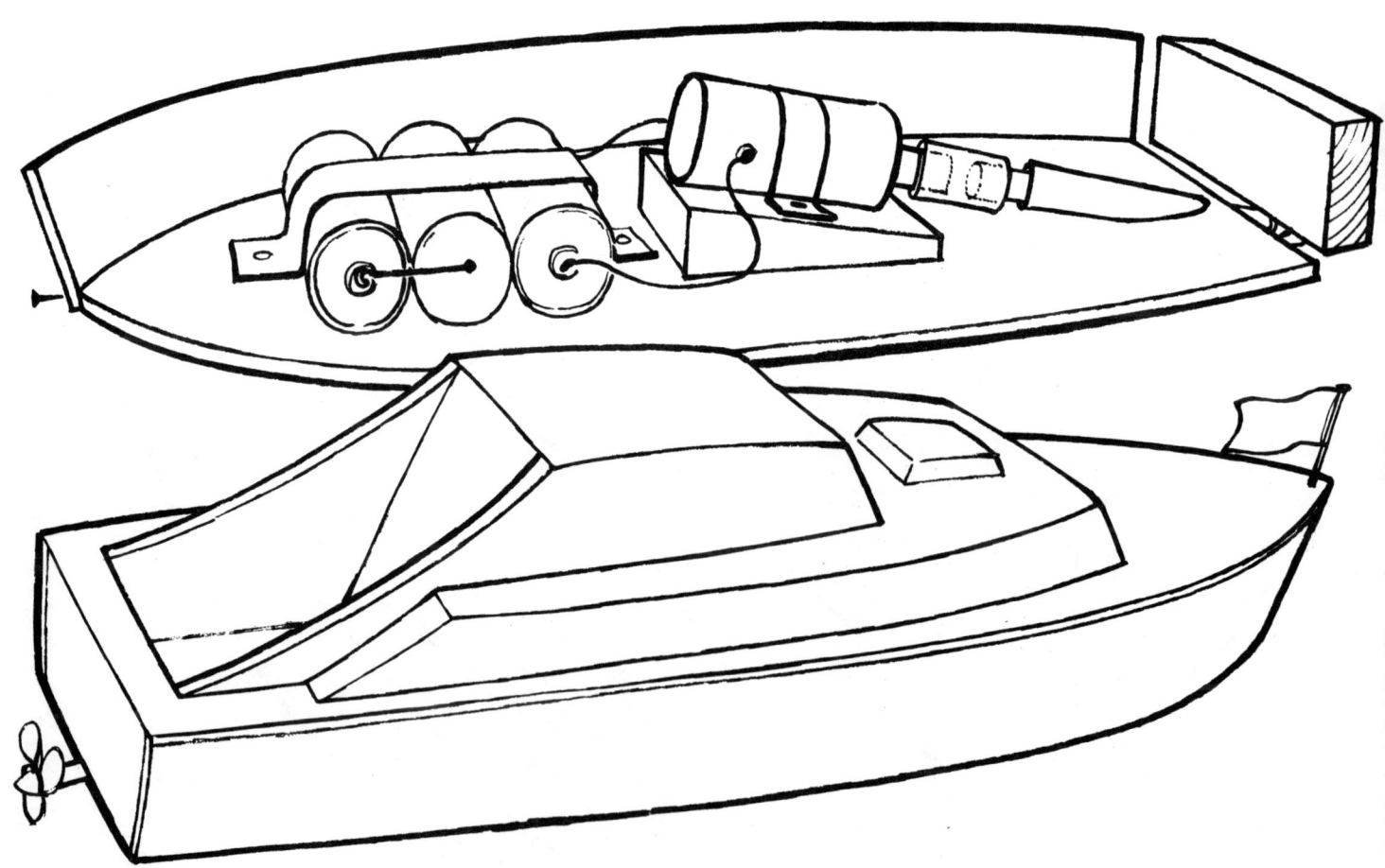

9
Fittings

Masts, booms, sails, and rigging are as important as the hull. We use dowel rod for masts and booms and brass eyelets on the sail to string that to the masts and booms. These eyelets make good portholes if hammered into the hull. Nails left proud in the deck and strung with wire or string make the handrail.

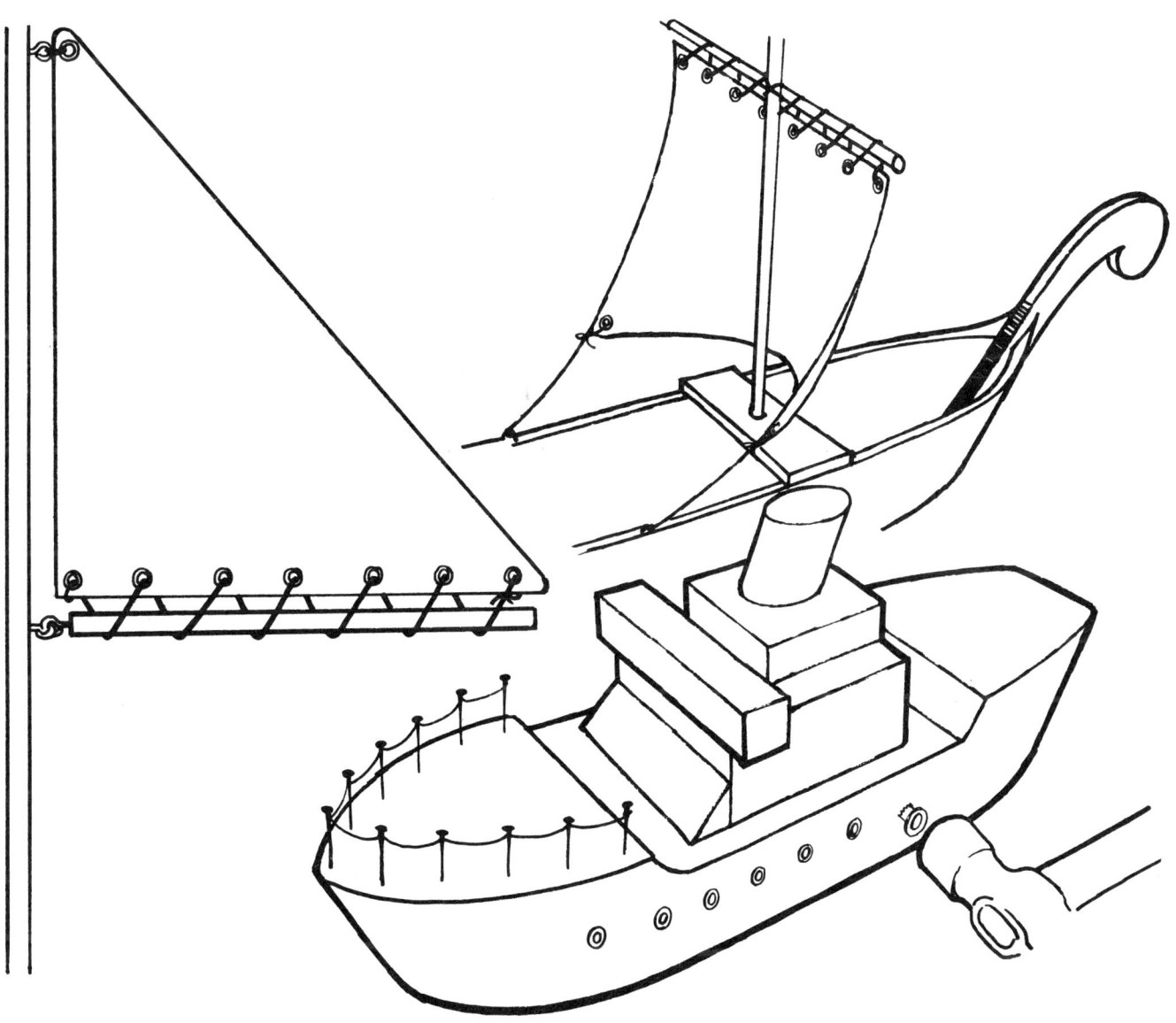

10
Tinplate Steamer

A good way to use old large tins is to cut them up into sheets and make them into boat hulls. It's best to practice with a paper pattern beforehand, though. Copper tubing is coiled and soldered into the boat, with its ends in the water. When the coil is heated (by either a small alcohol burner or paraffin lamp (see page 54), the boat steams forward.

  Materials: tinplate, solder, copper tubing.

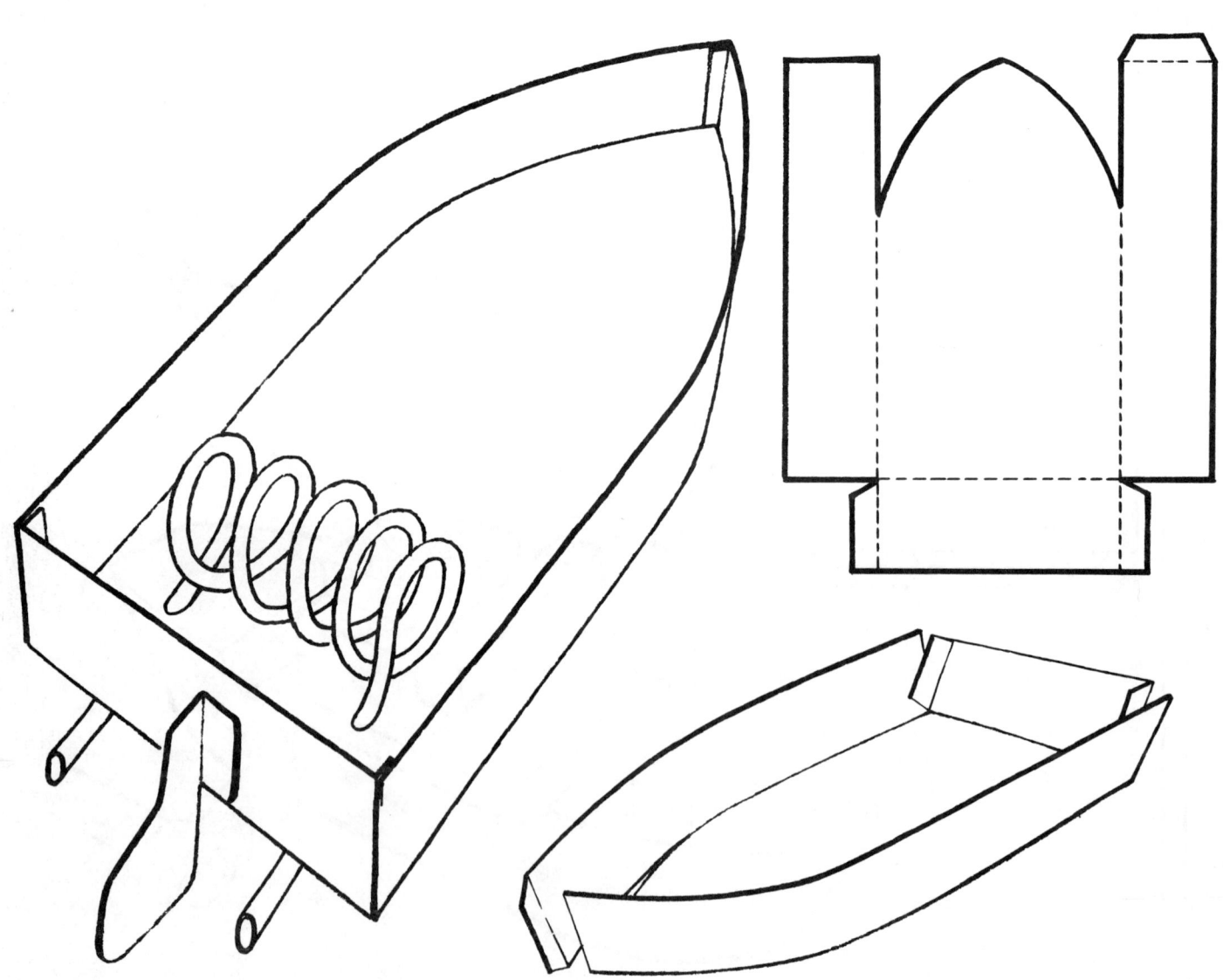

GAMES

Games made in Summerhill range from dominoes to pinball machines, and, apart from the latter, they seem to be made mainly for parents and younger brothers and sisters. Autumn term is the favorite time to make games as Christmas is in everyone's mind, and games are a real fun thing to give as presents. Afterwards they can be used by yourself as well.

One of my favorites is the jigsaw puzzle; I often make several for friends. Sometimes, instead of using a picture, I use large letters in the form of a message that is usually comic and gets everyone guessing as the puzzle nears completion, or even a riddle so that when the puzzle is complete there's still something to ponder.

13
Dominoes (Branding)

Domino sets are a popular item, as they are quickly made and involve branding the dots and cross bars on the pieces. Branding consists of heating to red heat pieces of steel or metal rods (that have wooden handles to insulate them) in the gas torch and burning wood with them in the desired pattern. Many interesting shapes and textures can be achieved using this method, which is spectacular when clouds of smoke issue out from under the rod and fill the air with pinewood smell.

Materials: softwood or hardwood rectangular strip.

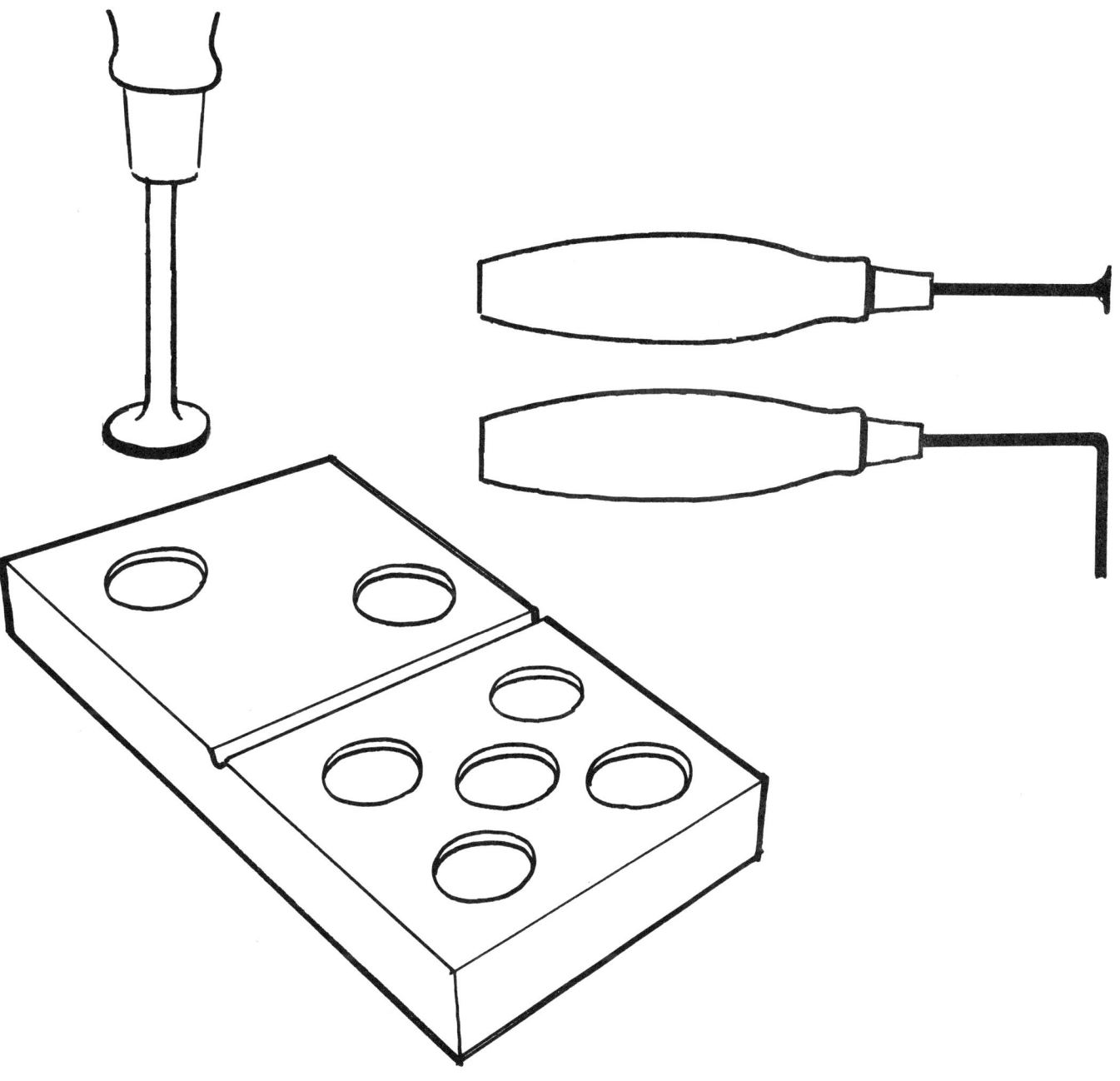

14
Solitaire (Pegboard Game)

An interesting game, the idea being to start with a full board except for the center hole and by jumping pegs over pegs to remove them, ending up with one peg in the middle. Dowel rod pegs or marbles can be used for markers.

Materials: softwood or hardwood board, dowel rod or marbles.

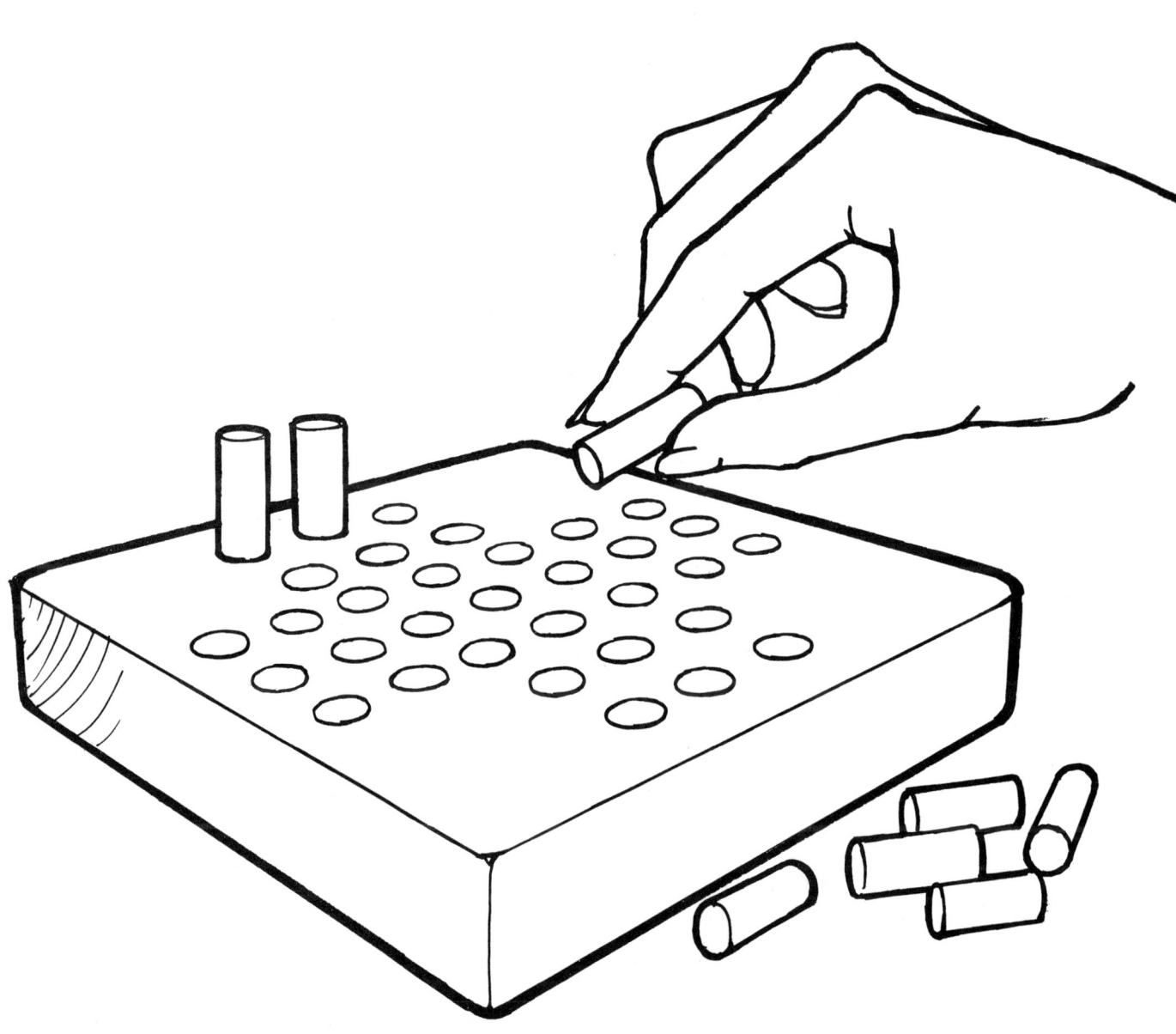

15
Dice Game

The dice are made from squared section wood, with dots branded on. The game is like snakes and ladders, only the squares on the board have your own slogans, moves, etc., on them.

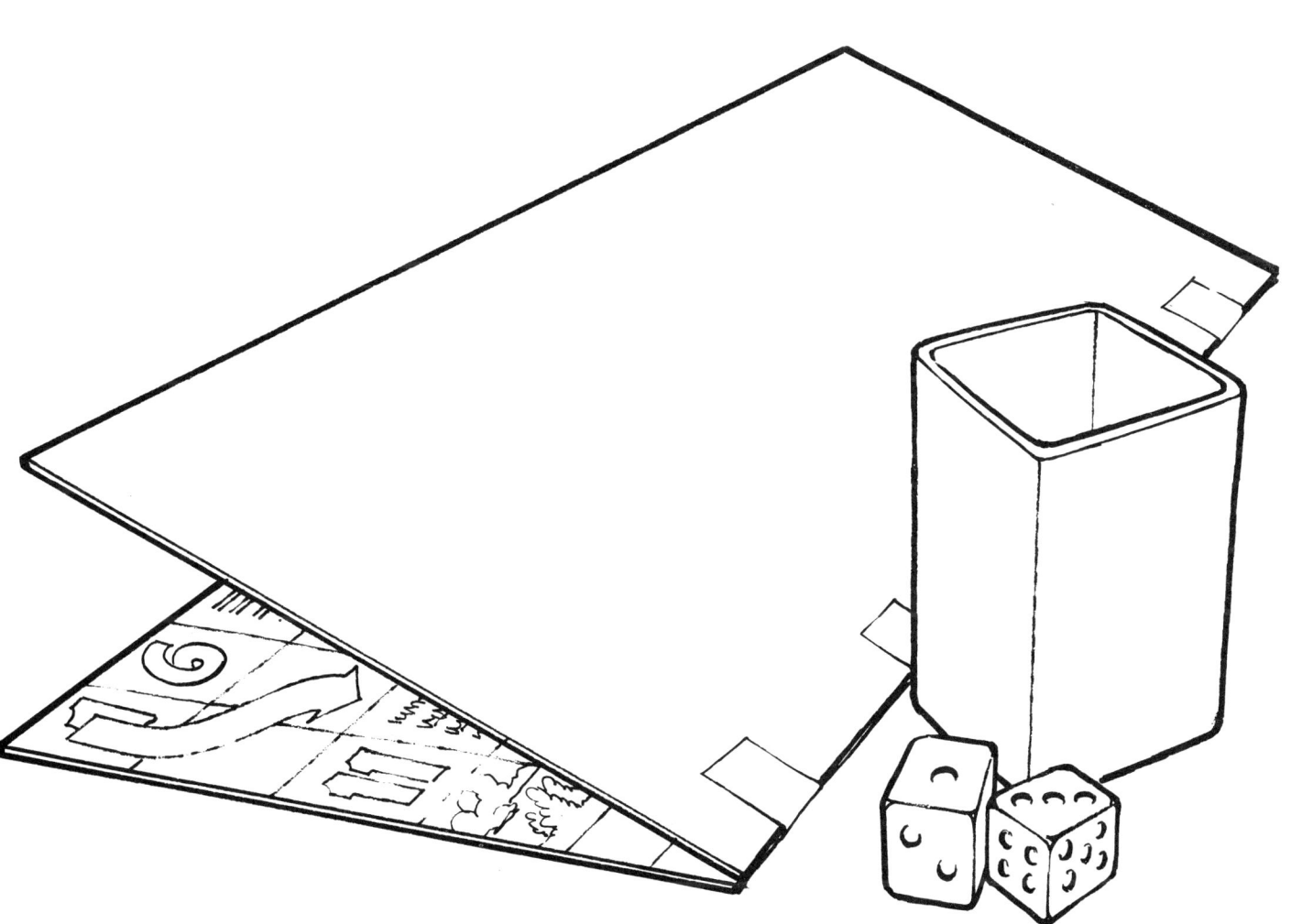

16
Jigsaw Puzzle

Jigsaw puzzles are especially good if the pieces are cut into irregular shapes—it makes the whole thing more interesting. Also a good idea is to use photographs, magazine pictures, or your own paintings for the subject of the puzzle.

Materials: hardboard or thin plywood, picture or photograph.

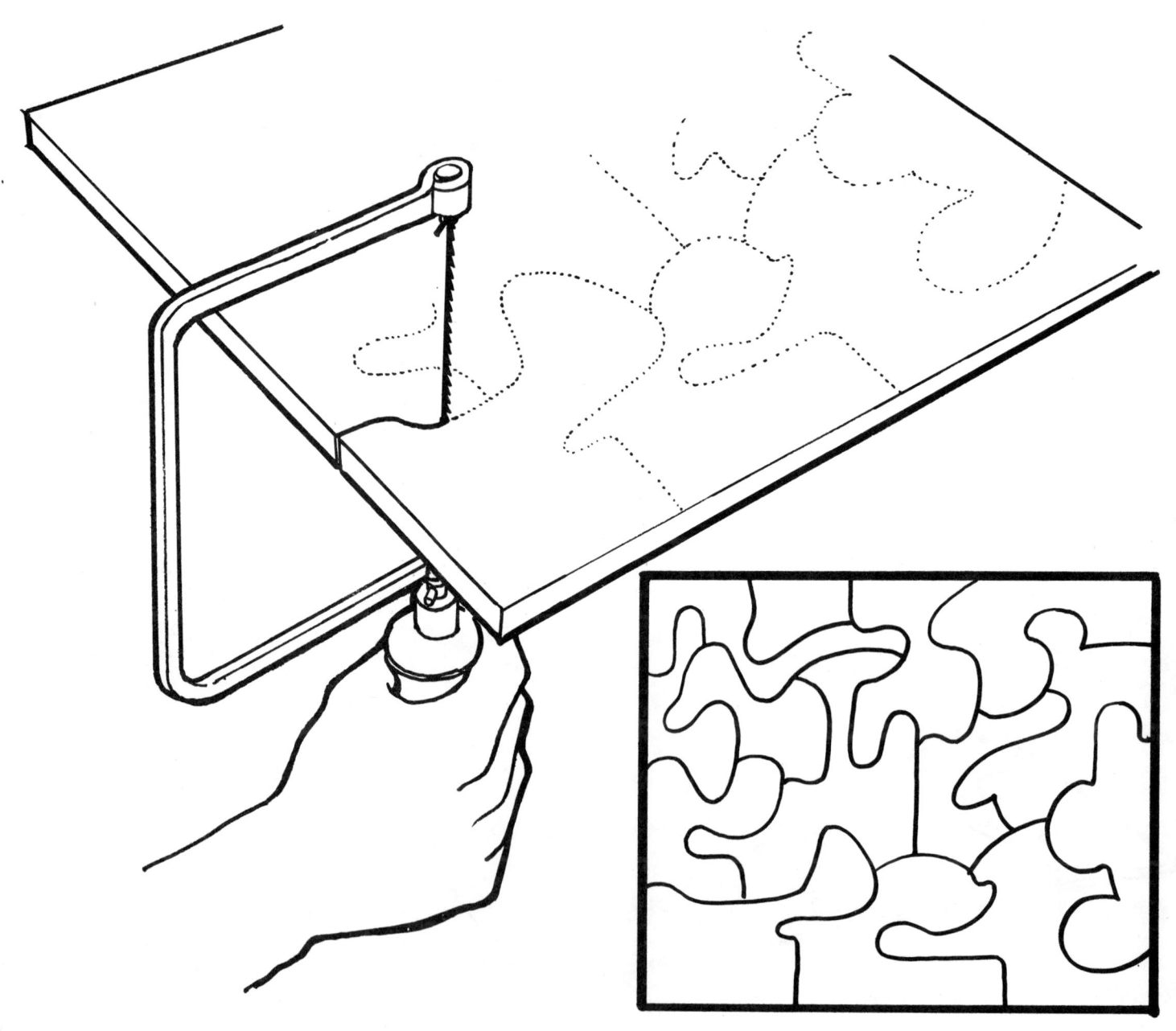

17
Cube Game

A single open pine box in which cubes of wood have to be fitted (some glued together). More complicated games when the cubes are two or three layers thick.
  Materials: pinewood box, softwood or hardwood cubes.

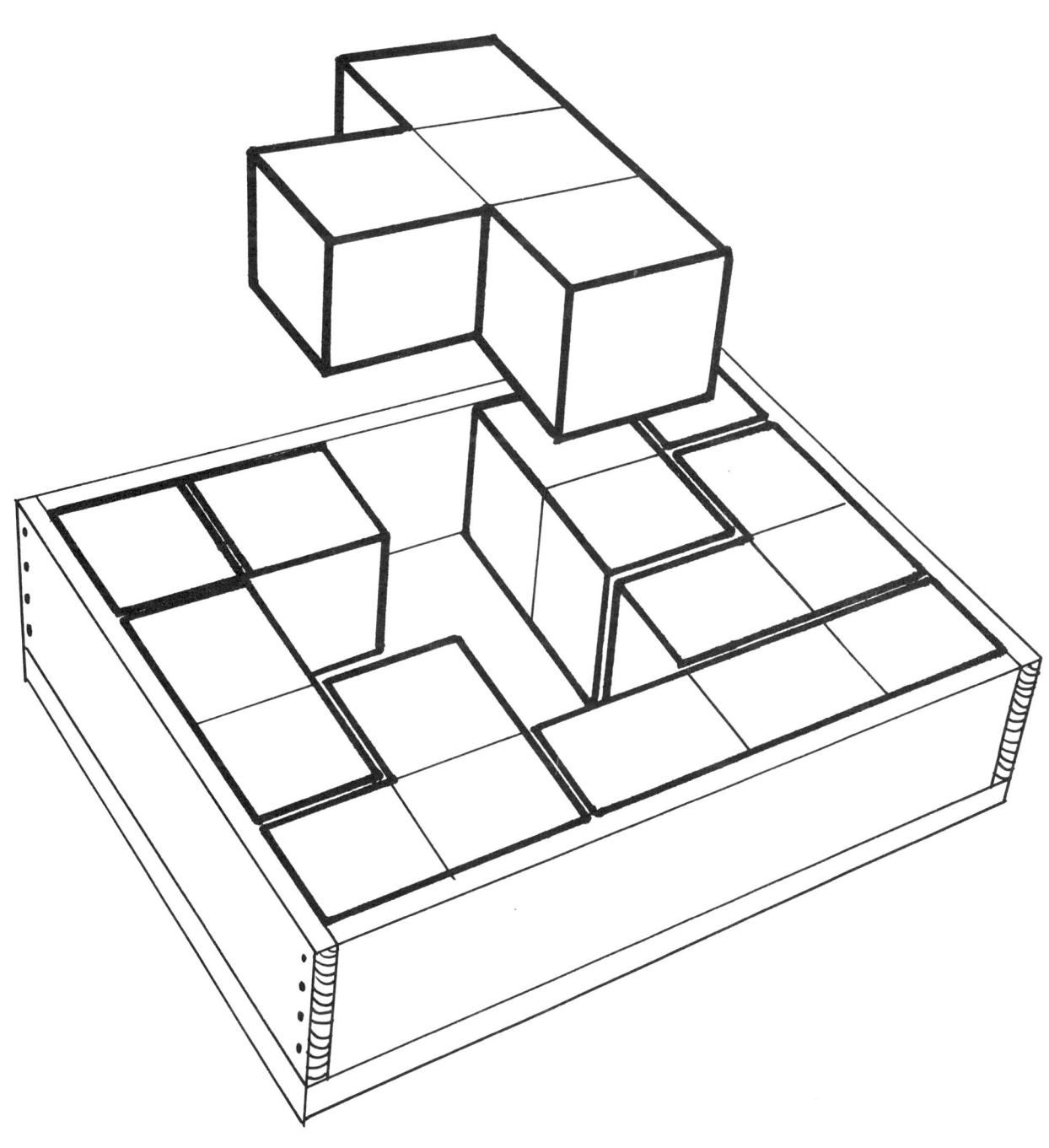

18
Cube Puzzle

I recently made a six-in-one puzzle using cubes. I cut up pictures to paste on the set of cubes, doing this six times—but first shuffling the cubes, with any blank face up, each time. It's fun to use photographs. Solving the puzzles afterwards sounds easy, however . . .

Materials: pinewood box, softwood or hardwood cubes, pictures.

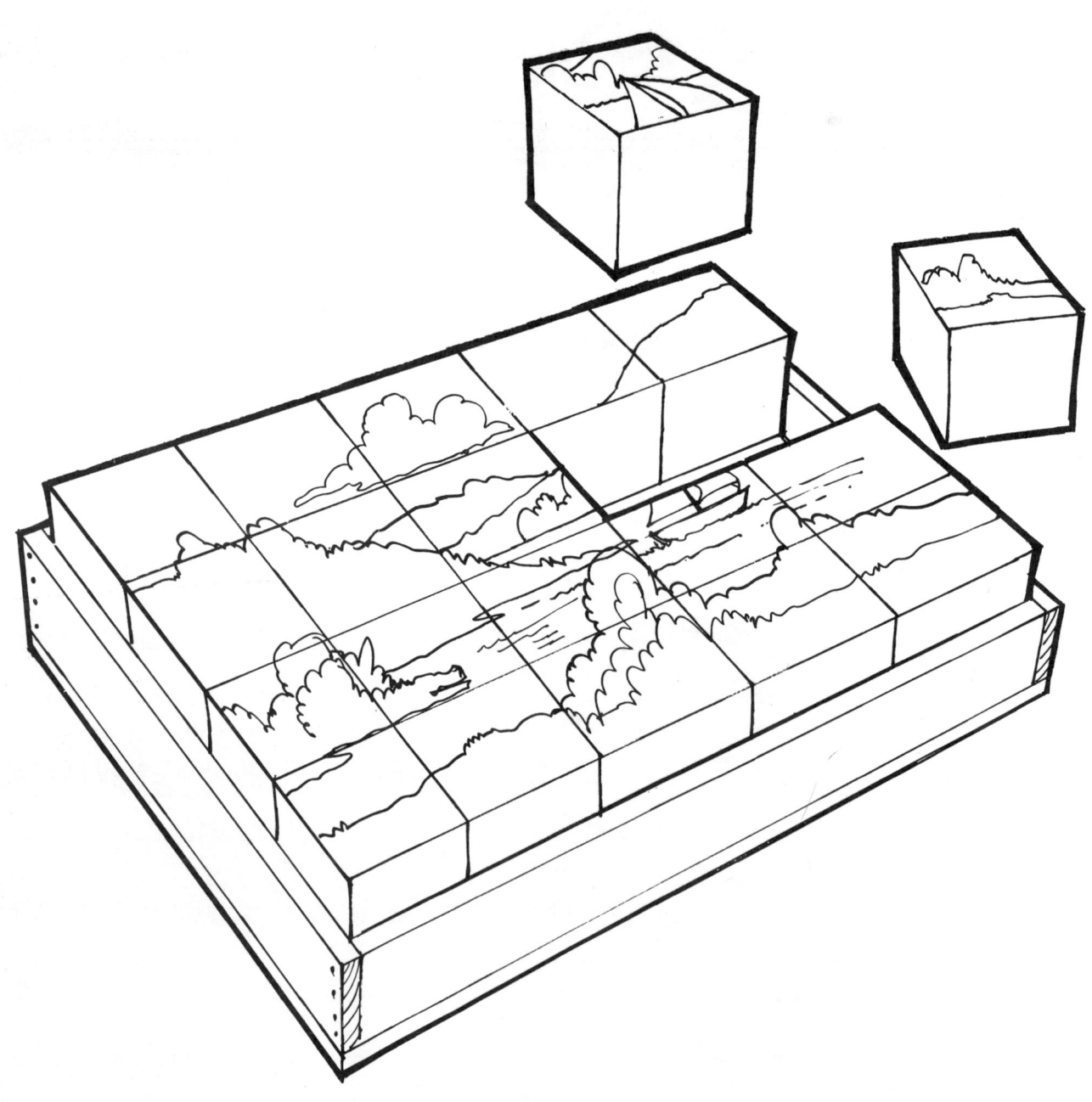

19
Ball Maze

A marble has to get through the maze without falling through one of the traps. Bottom of box can have half circles on it or the maze part can be set up in a gimbal arrangement.
 Materials: pine board, hardboard.

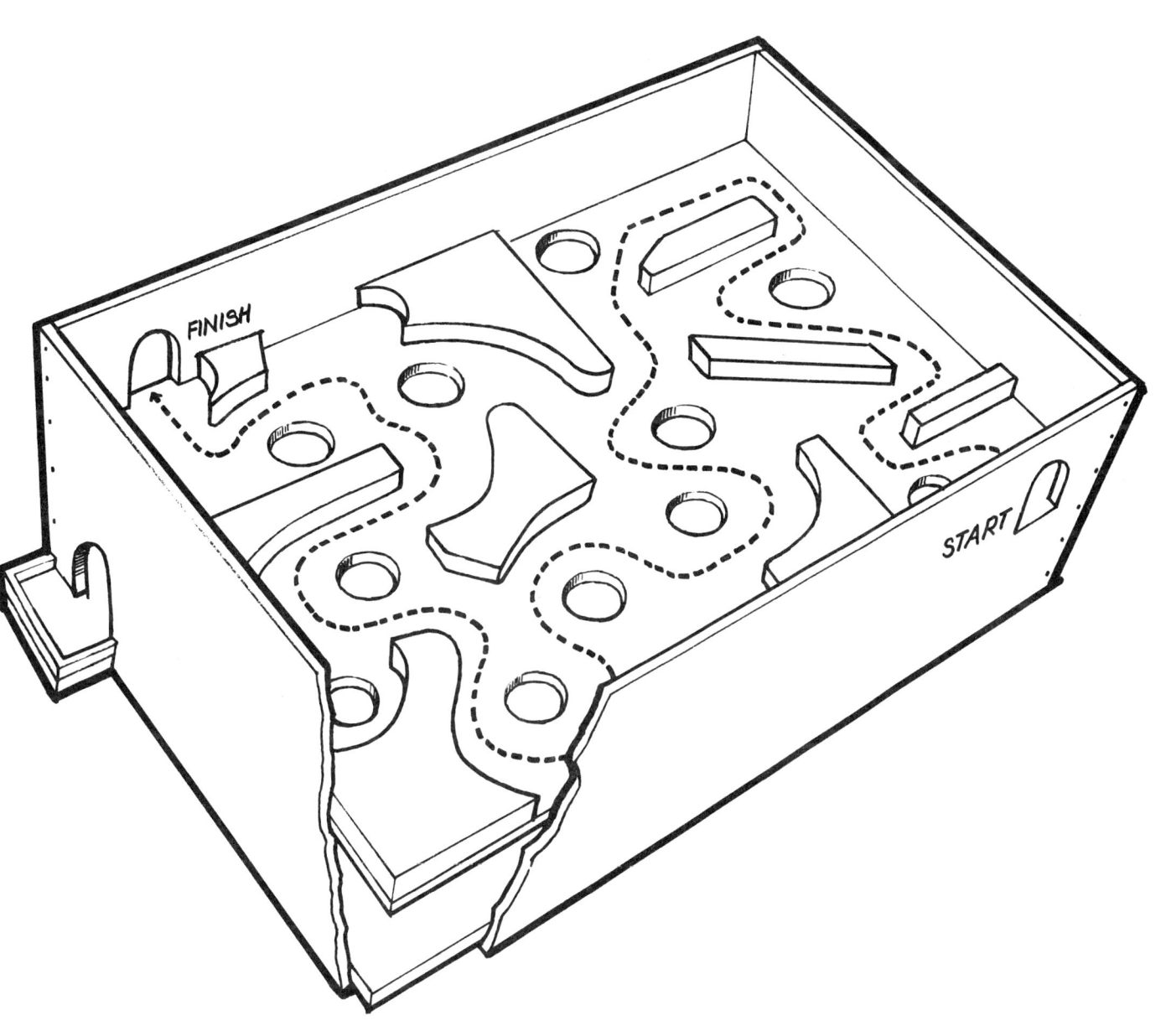

20
Pinball Machine

This can be simple or complex. Elastic bands serve as bumpers for the marble. (Old cut up cycle inner tubes are a good substitute.) Flippers at the bottom can be worked directly by the player or by mechanical means from the side of the board. Artists can have a field day decorating the playing area.

Materials: chipboard base, hardboard surround, pine fittings.

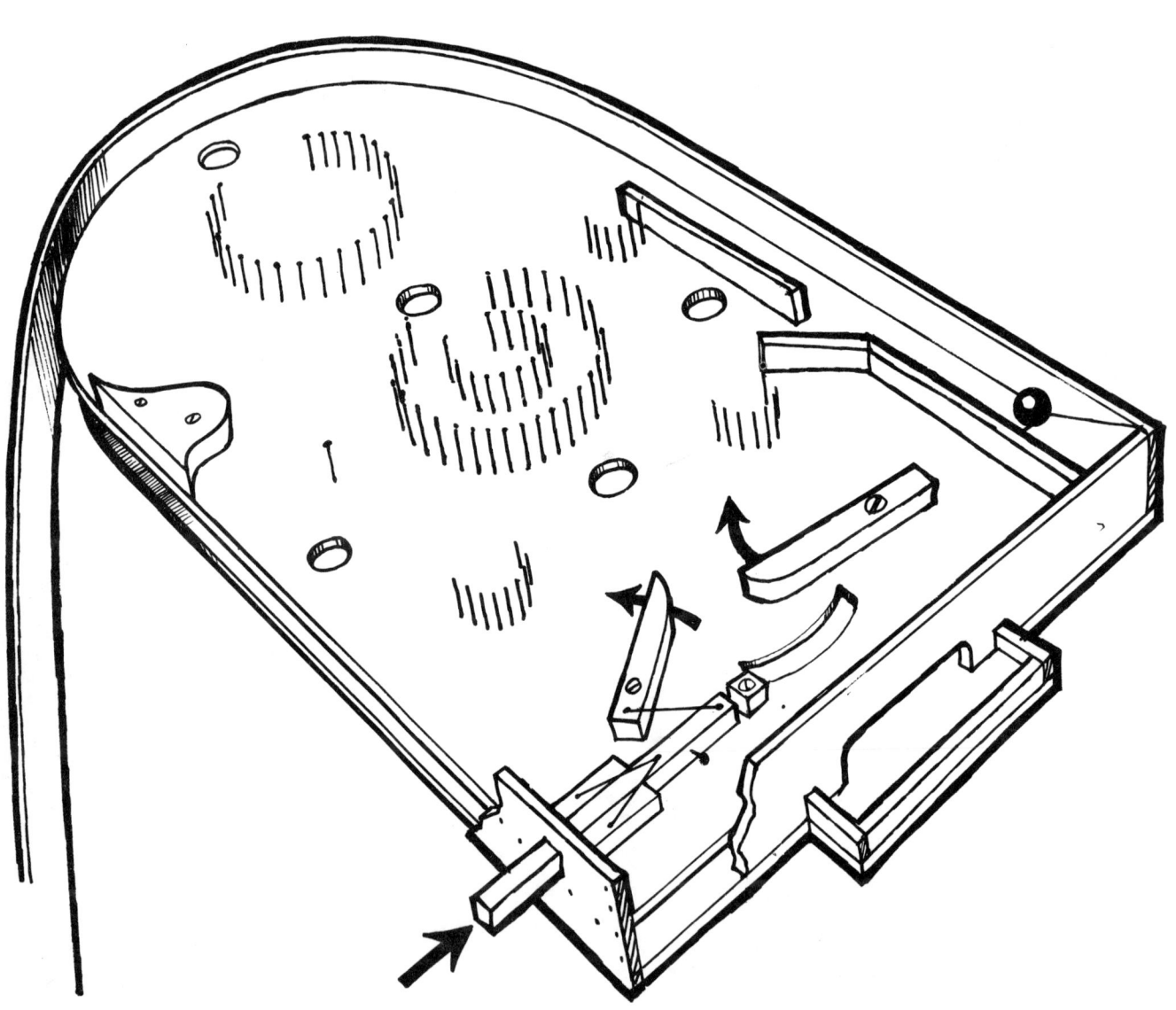

21
Billiard Table

This is a miniature version using marbles for the balls and dowel rods for cues. One-half-inch plywood gives a smooth base and an old sheet a fair playing surface.

Materials: plywood base, pinewood surround, dowel cue, large marbles (or ball bearings).

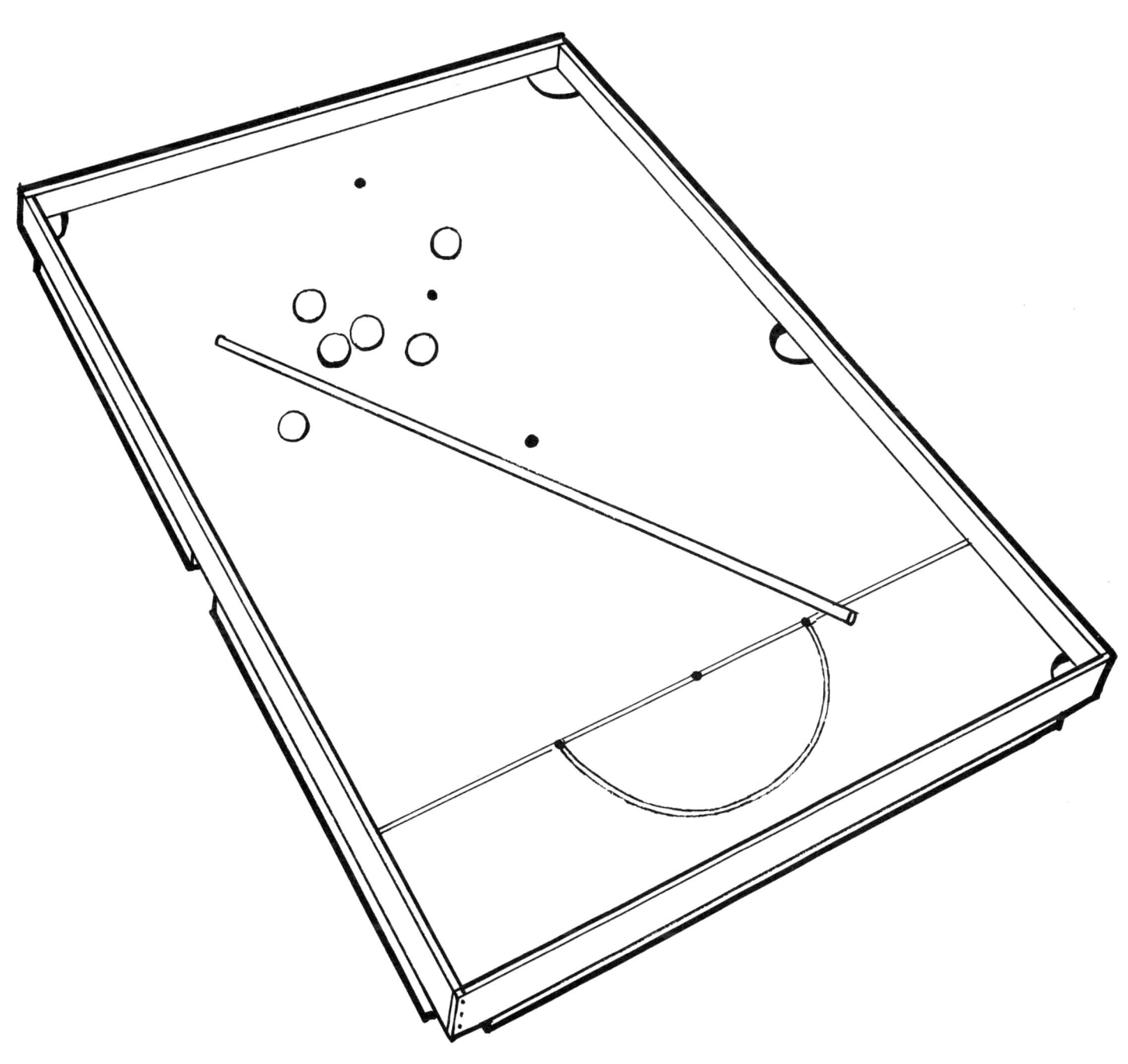

22
Chess Set

An interesting proposition when the pieces have to be designed as well as made. The playing board can be made by drawing squares on plywood and coloring alternate areas or by cutting wood veneers into squares and gluing them on alternately. A really substantial board can be made out of small cubes glued together alternating end grain and side grain (see page 93, chopping board). Chess pieces can be made from a large piece of dowel rod cut into sections, one set colored.

Materials: multimedia—clay, wood, metals, plastic, etc.

23
Whizzer

One or several can be made quickly and look good when incorporating a pattern. (Provides an easy way to show that the rainbow colors make white when blended.)
 Materials: plastic or hardboard.

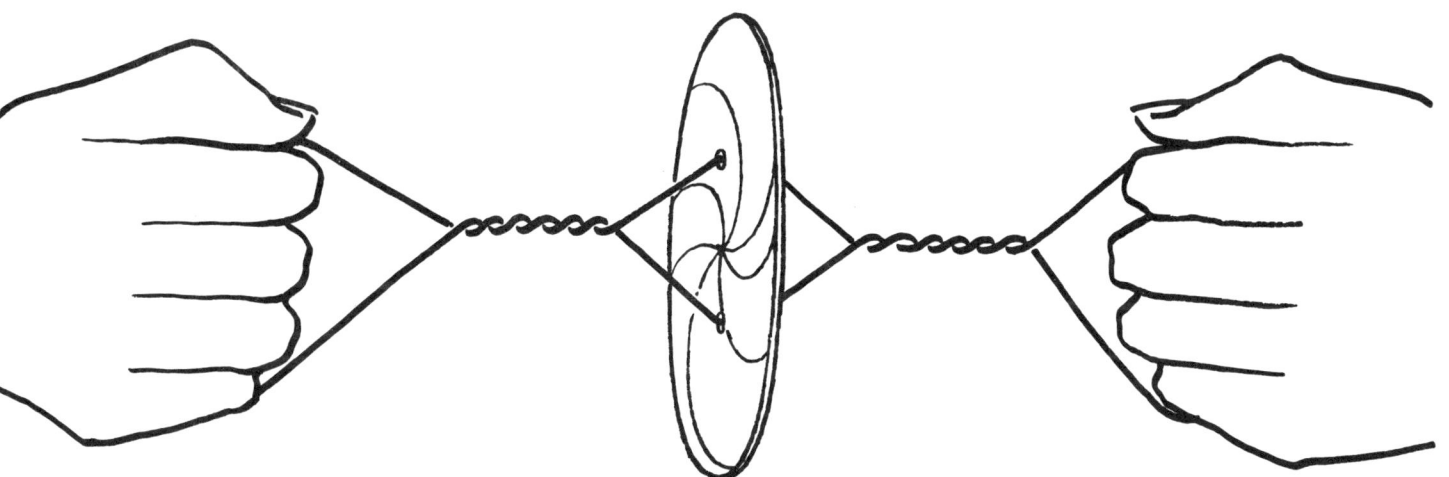

Spinning Tops

Turned on the lathe and painted. There is an art in keeping one going. The whip is a piece of dowel with a leather thong on the end.

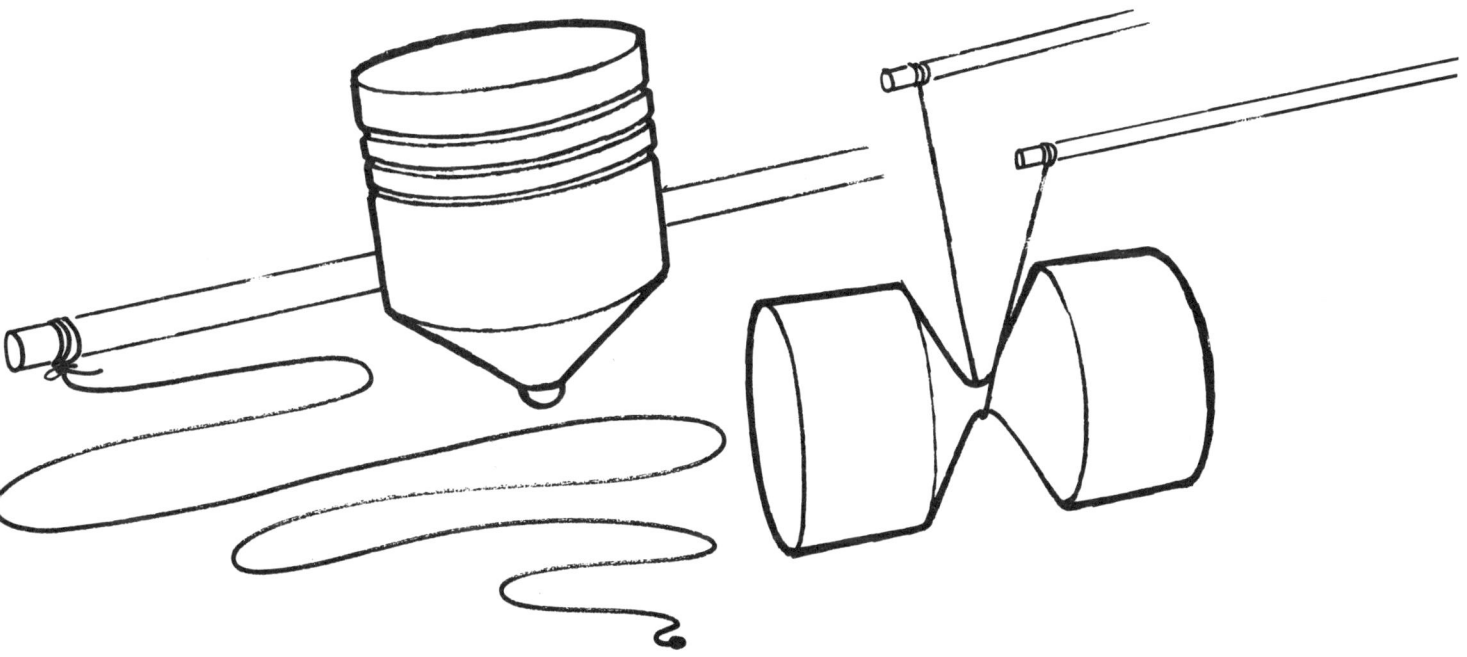

24
Construction Game

Can be made from wood and dowel rod or metal cubes and rods. People play with this compulsively if it is left lying around. It is interesting to set problems like trying to balance all the pieces on one block, or to see who can make the longest or most compact structure using all the pieces.

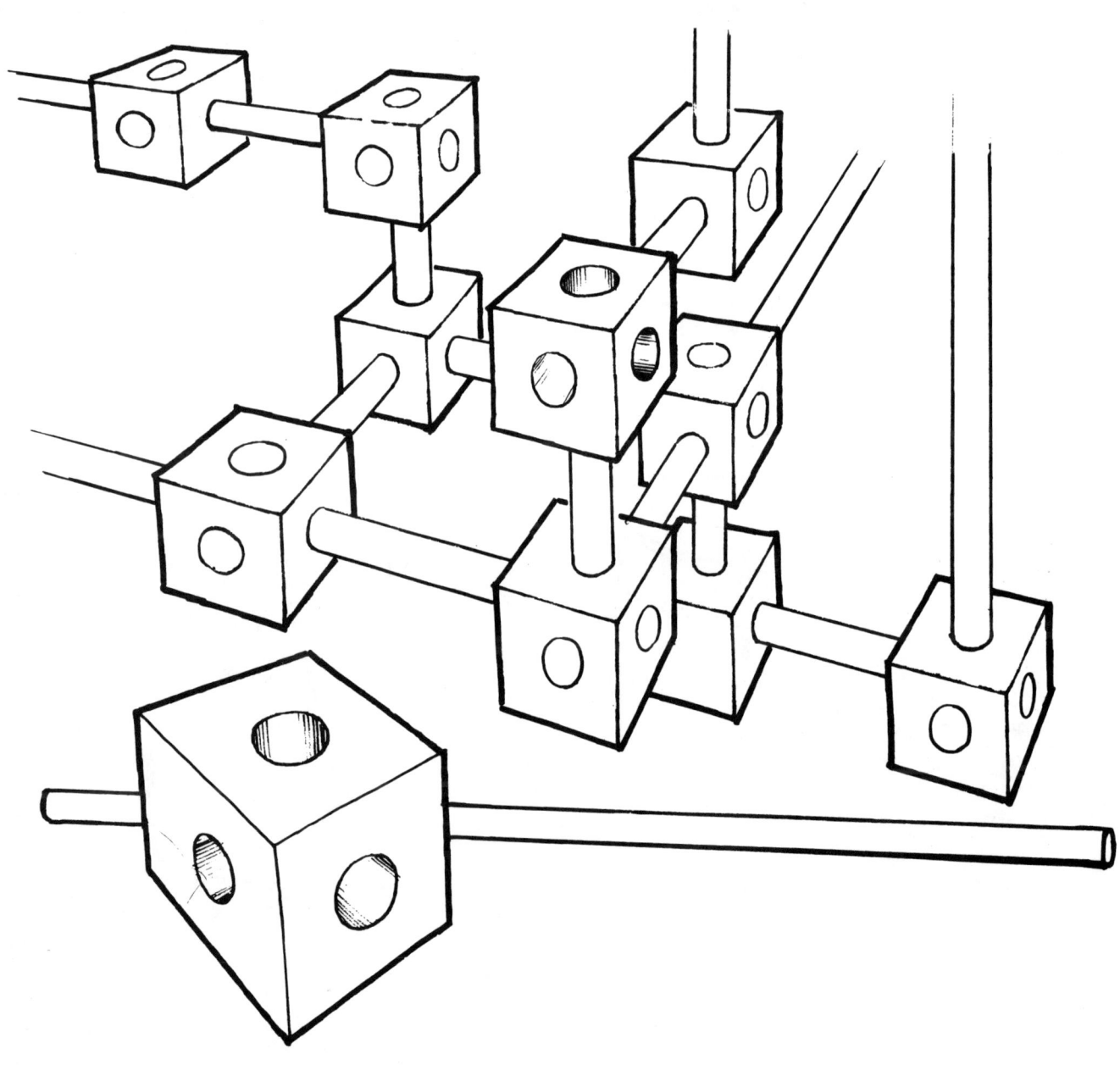

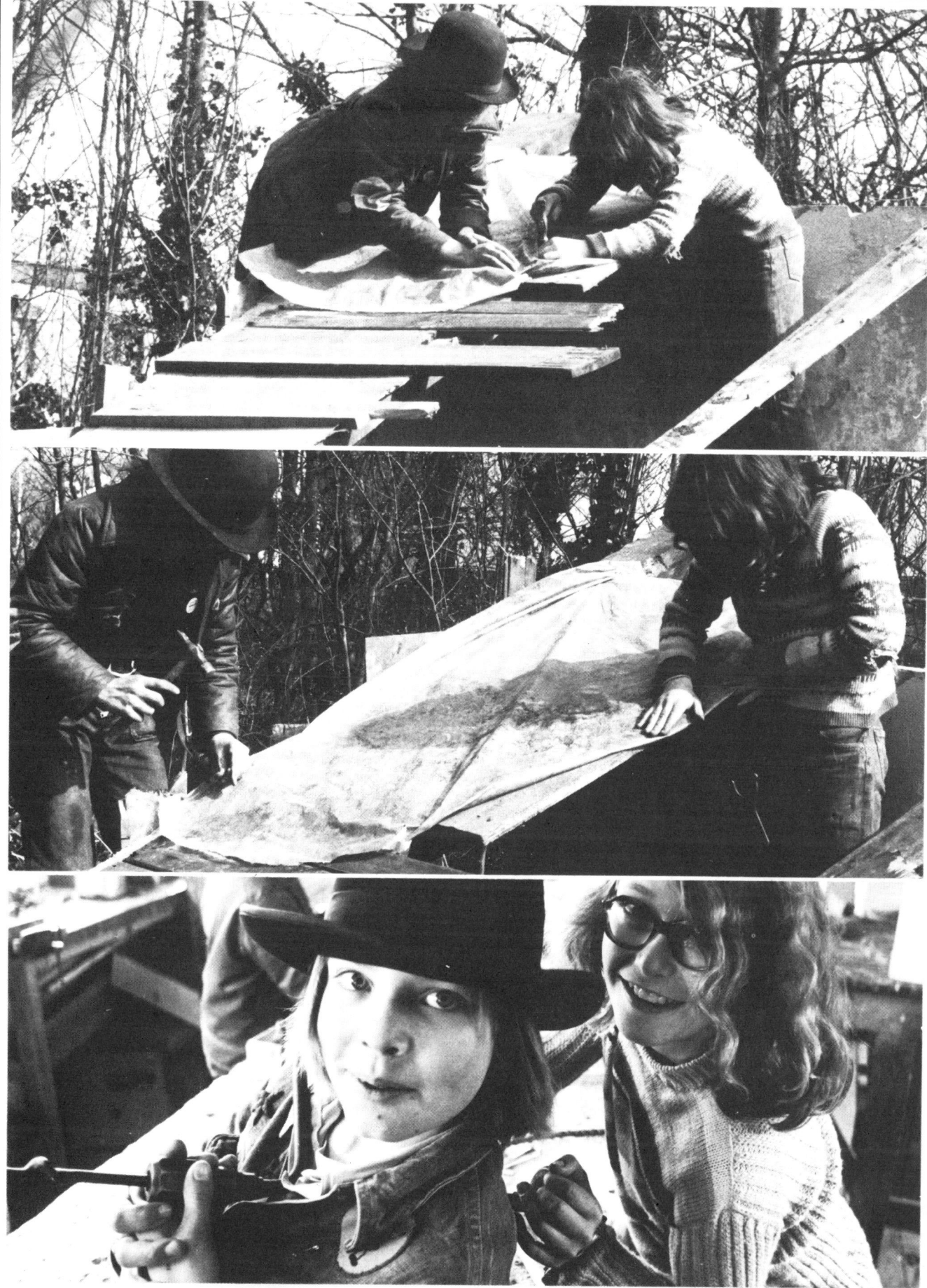

GUNS

Guns are made at a very steady rate in the workshop. They seem to fulfill a fantasy need in children, especially when at the playing-gangsters age. Normally perhaps only two or three are made per week, but when a war or gangster game is being organized (sometimes one goes on spasmodically for days), the rate of manufacture increases tenfold. The children in Summerhill don't seem to form permanent attachments to their guns, perhaps because they are easily made or because they are symbolic at the time and of no use afterward. At any rate, everyone seems to have a great deal of fun making and playing with them.

27
Revolver

This gun can be made in pine but particularly lends itself to plywood, which, after the outline has been cut out, can be paired layer by layer to feature things like the foresight and trigger. The revolving chamber is a piece of dowel pinned back and front so that it turns freely.

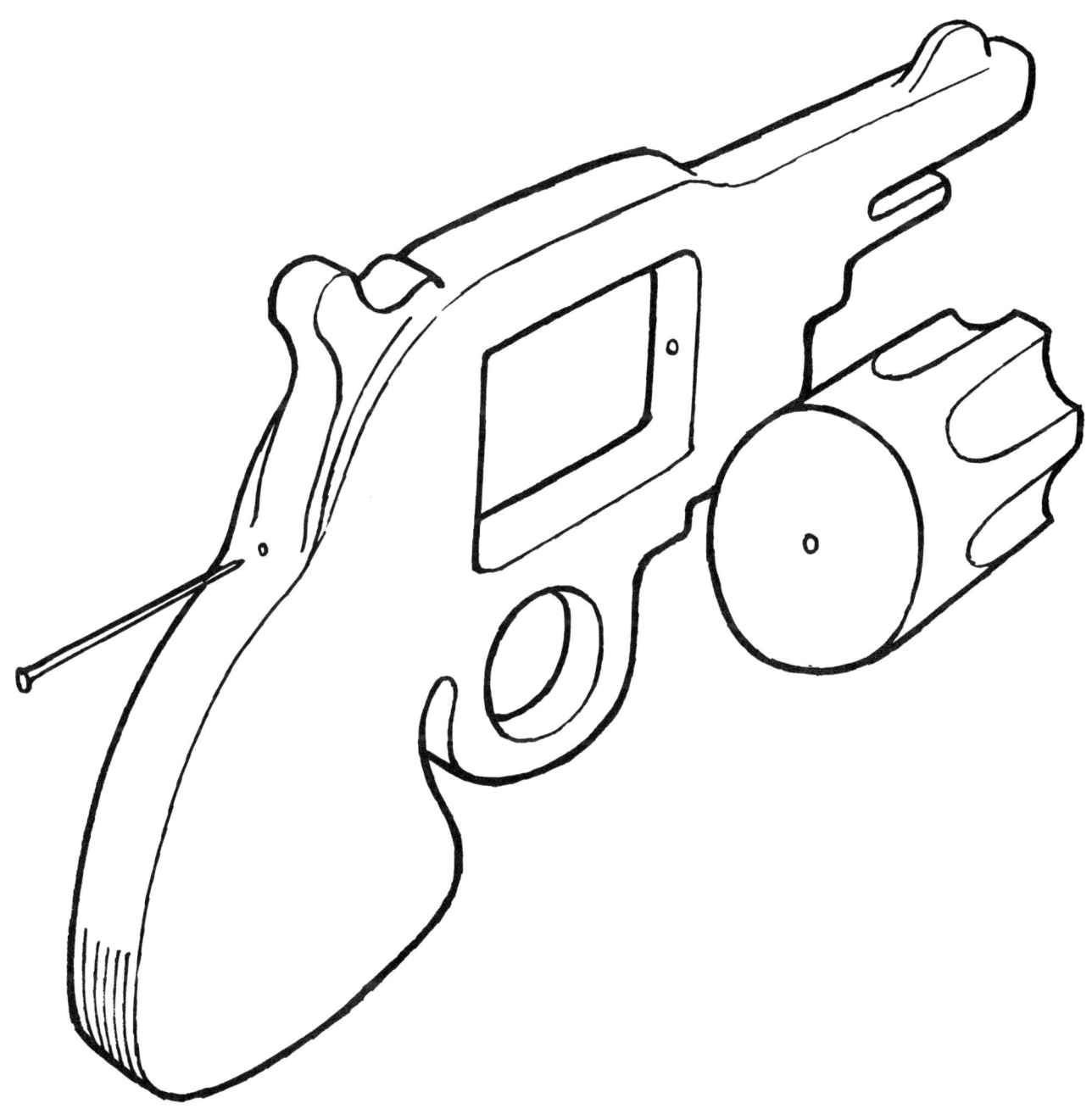

28
Cut-Out Guns

What I call outline guns are basically the cowboy six-shooter and the automatic. Drawn onto a piece of board, they are easily cut out using a coping saw. (For very young children a template might be useful.) Grips on the butt can be simulated by branding a criss-cross pattern on it.

Materials: softwood, chipboard, plywood.

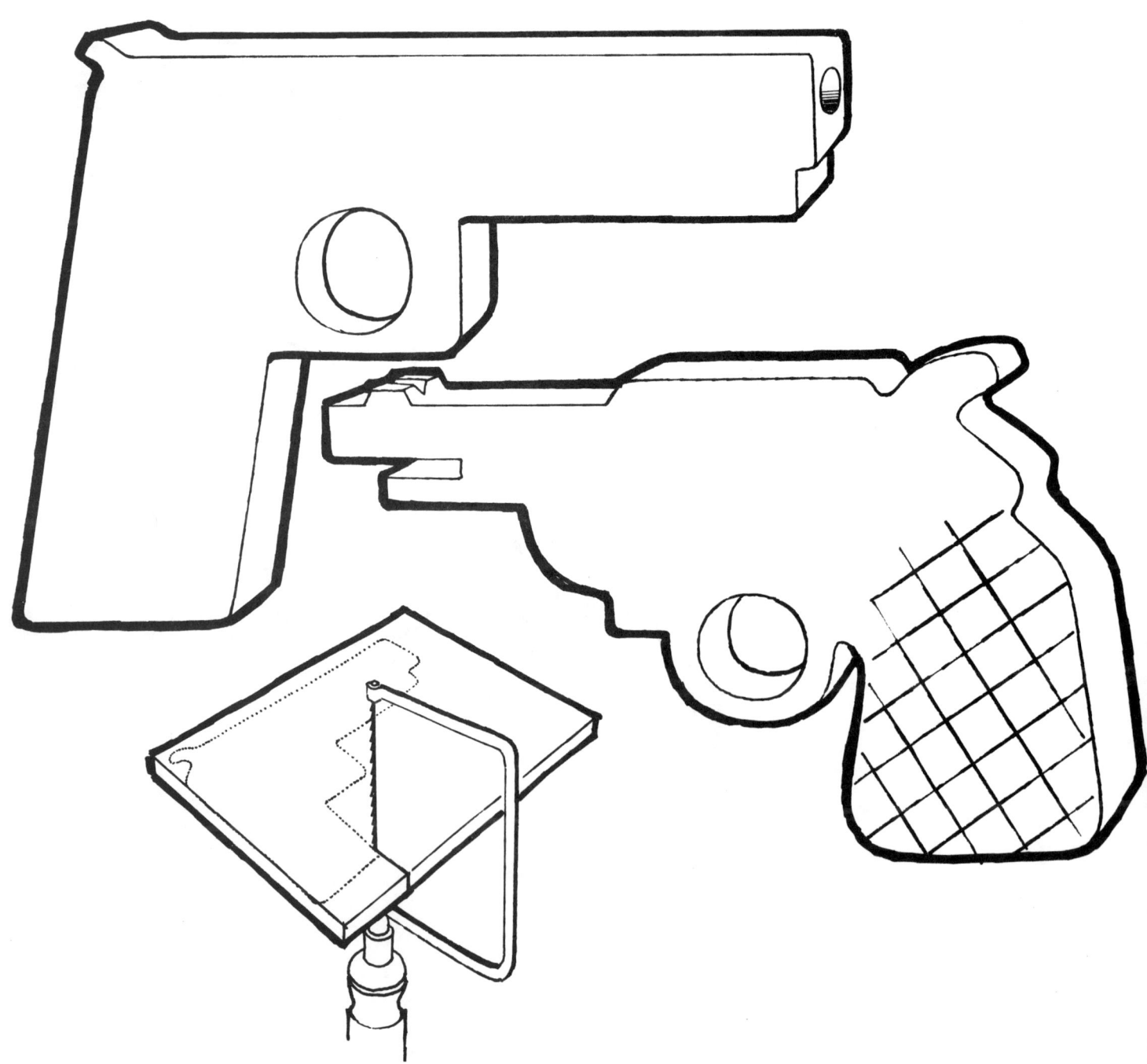

29
Tube Guns

The tube pistol and rifle are a step further in realism. We use any old metal tube, usually off an old bicycle. The stock or handle is made from wood and the barrel held on by bands of tinplate, copper, or brass screwed into the wood. These guns usually look good and last longer than all wood versions.

   Materials: metal tubing, pine board.

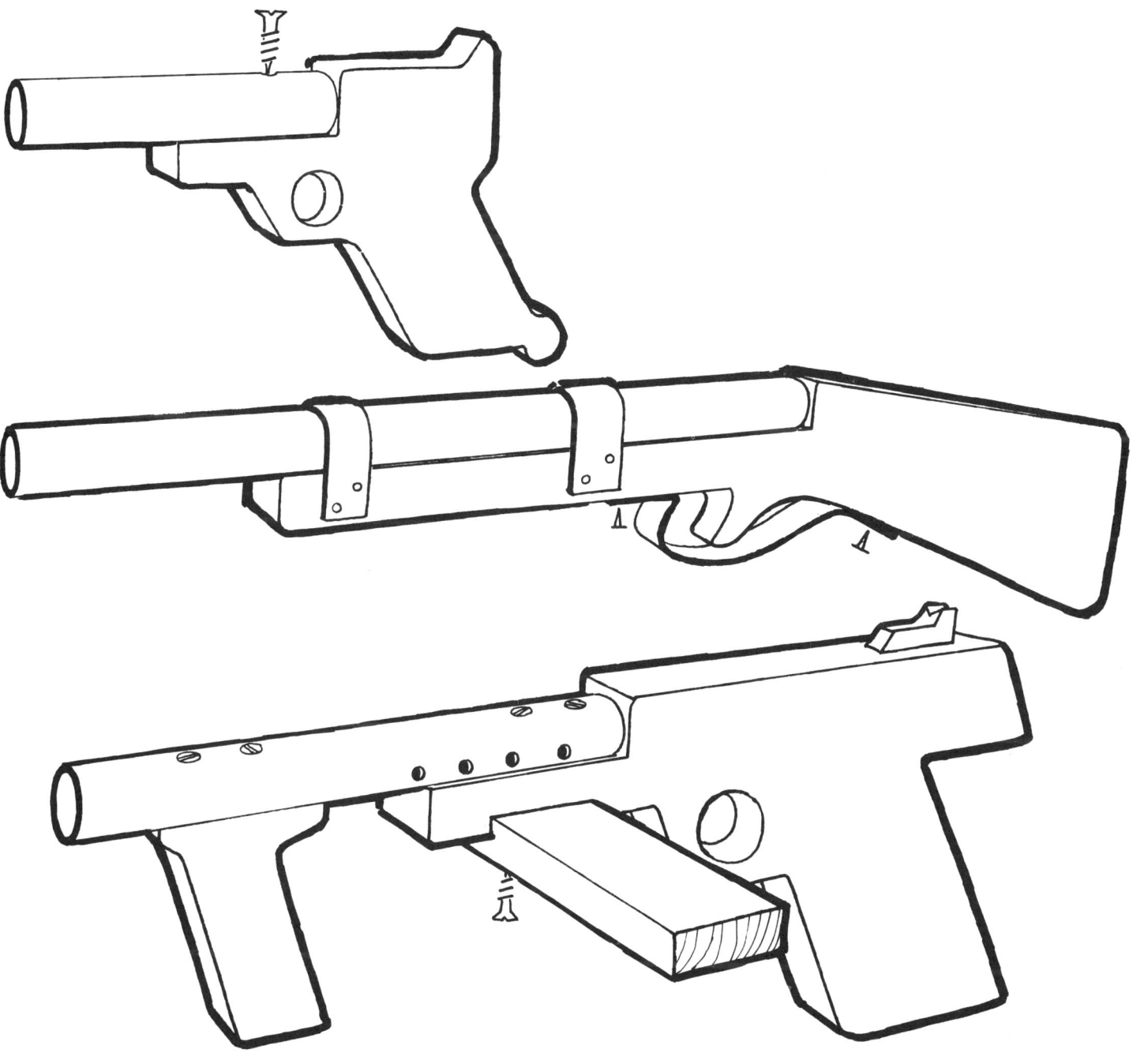

30
Extras

To overcome the old groan about heroes in films having a shoot-out and never reloading, the kids here developed their own quick reload clips that snap on and off in an instant. Good for the traditional tommy gun as well as automatic pistols. An imitation of General Thompson's circular clockwork magazine, holding 200 rounds, is popular.

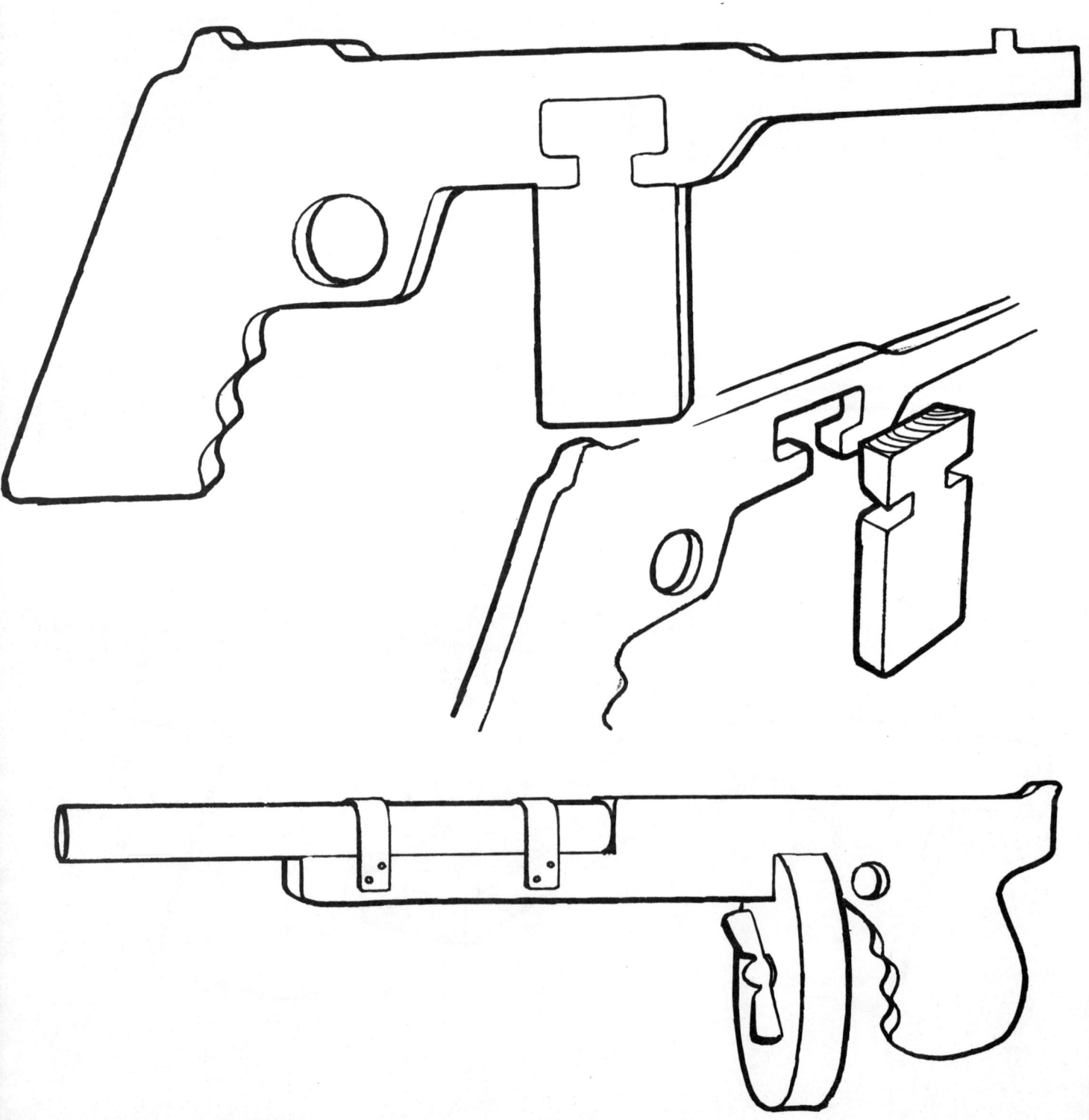

AIR MACHINES

35
Vintage Airplanes

Multiple winged airplanes with propellers still seem to hold more fascination for children than modern jets. Perhaps this is because it's easy to see why they work, whereas jets are a bit of a mystery. The fuselage is usually made from section wood and the wings from thin planking. Propellers are tinplate, cut out and twisted as shown.

Materials: pine board, section tinplate.

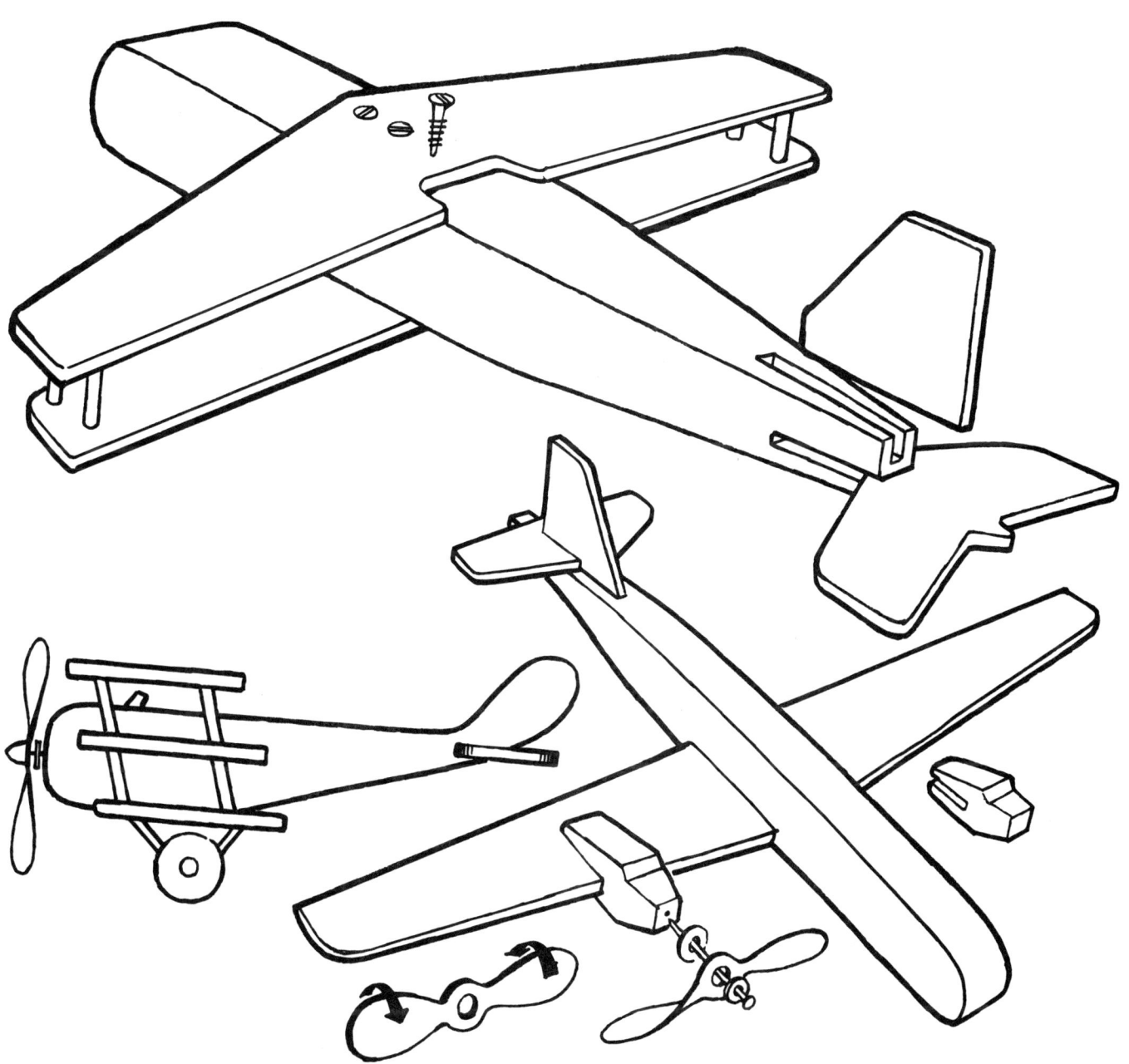

36
Propellers

A propeller is basically a center boss or block with a hole in the middle and half its ends cut away at 45° (or a slot) where the blades are attached. If a cycle hub is to be used as a bearing, then the boss has to be cut in half and reglued round the hub. It's best to experiment for yourself with angles and shapes for the blade; basically a longer blade will turn more slowly than a short one, etc.

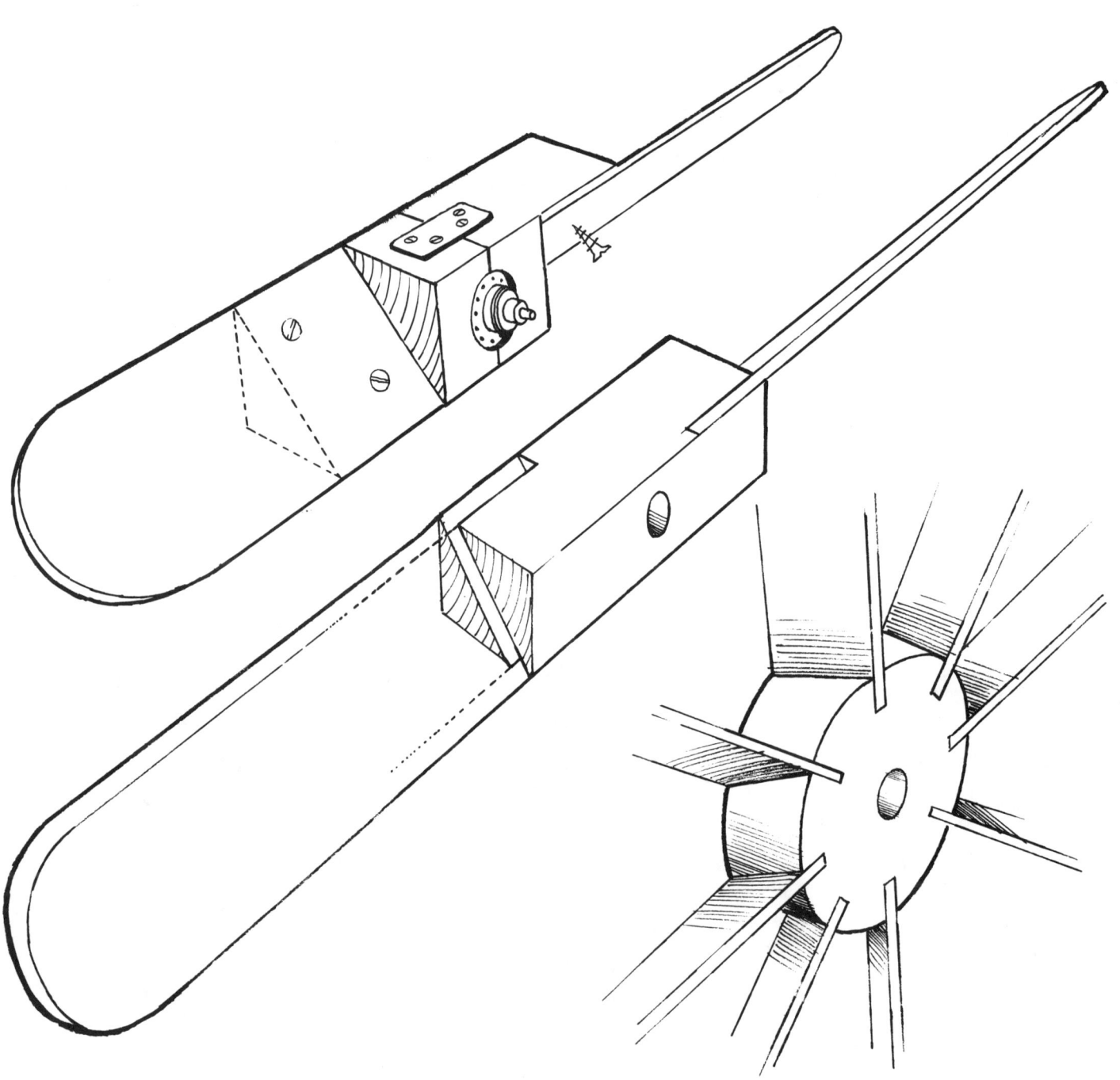

37
Basic Wind Machine or Windi

If ball bearings are not available, then a hole in the timber with a nail through it and two washers will work quite well. The number of propellers that can be put on one machine is strictly proportional to the inventiveness of the maker. Advertising space on the tail wind vane can, of course, be rented or else slogans can be painted there, etc.

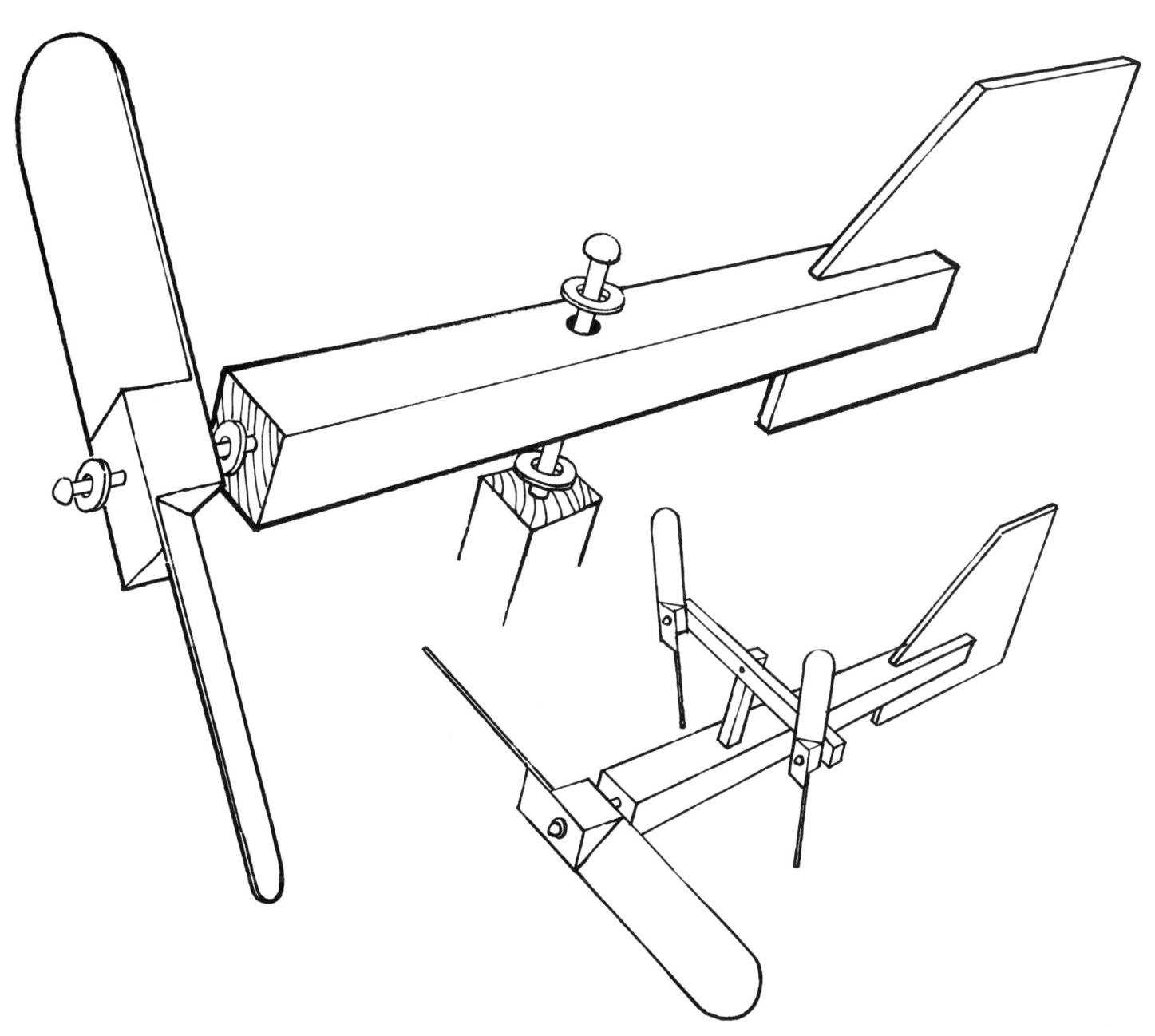

38
Cycle Front-Forks Windi

Cycle front forks, including head stock bearings, are a gift for the serious builder of windies, as these ball bearings respond immediately to changes in wind direction and speed. It is quite important to mount the bearings so that they are both horizontally and vertically true, otherwise their performance is impaired. If it isn't sufficient for the windi to simply turn in the wind and some sort of work is required, there are several possibilities. I attached a propeller to an automobile generator and got it to turn in the wind (a force-nine gale actually). I was hoping to feed the resultant electricity through the car voltage regulator and so charge up a battery. It's an interesting project that I haven't completed yet, as the generator has to be turned much faster than the wind speed around us to produce a useable voltage.

MIXED BAG

This last half of the book is taken up with the many varied items that don't fall naturally into any one category. You can browse through and find things like junk furniture from old car seats, jewelry, or handmade sandals. It's these sorts of projects that make up the other side of the workshop, not necessarily day to day items but things that get made occasionally or for a special need.

41
Land Racer

A model airplane engine and propeller can be used as a motive force for a wheeled vehicle. It's really very interesting trying to get the whole thing to go properly. Some sort of guidance system is usually necessary so that hazards can be negotiated.

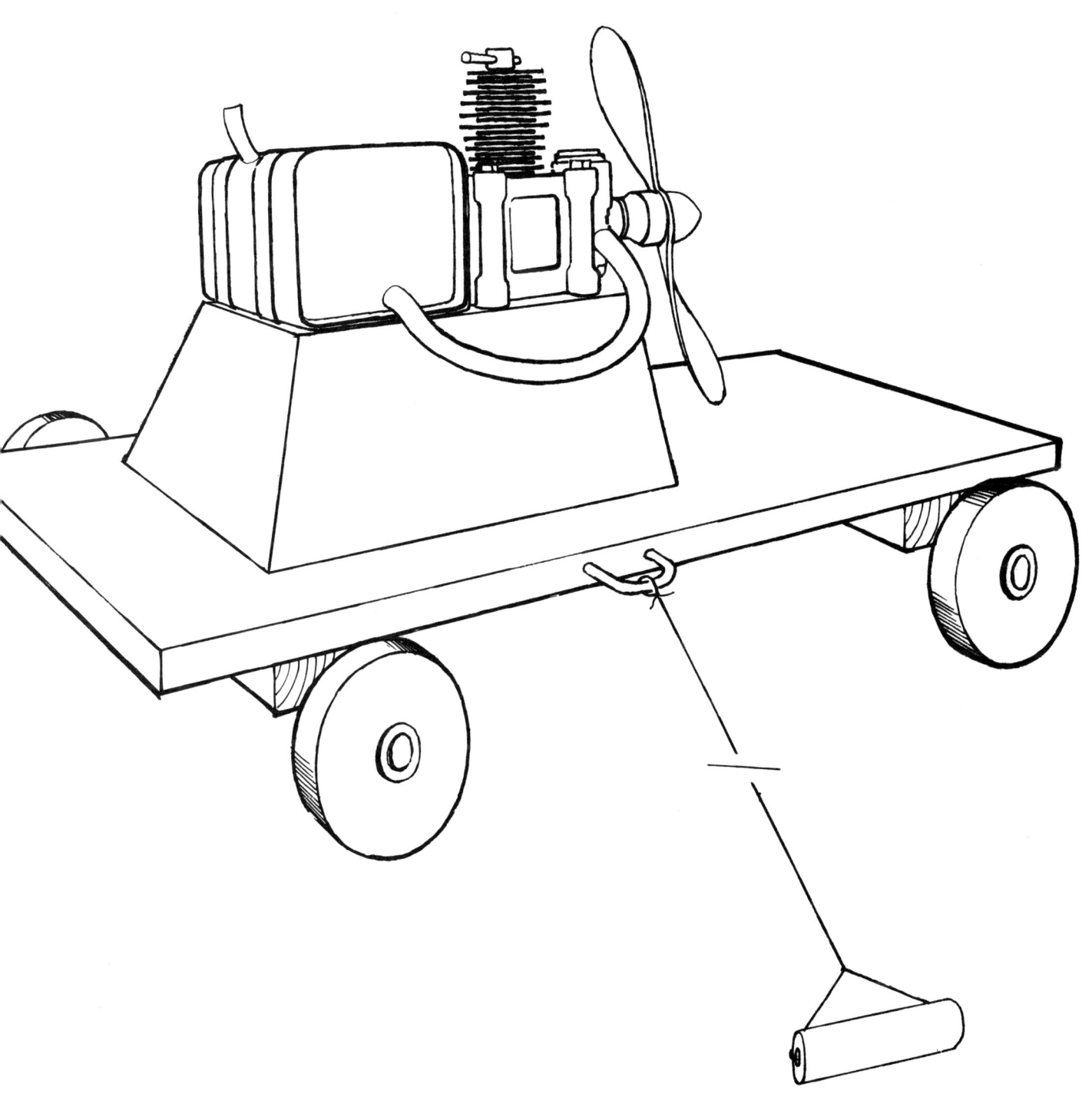

43
Thread-Spool Tanks

These developed quite quickly from ordinary thread spools with elastic bands through the middle, to larger versions of the same, turned on the wood lathe and powered by superstrong elastic. The latter versions had all sorts of aids, like rows of nail heads around the outside to give extra grip. Assault courses were built for them to go over, and pushing matches were regular events to see whose tank had the most power and grip.

Materials: thread spool or turned pinewood spool, candle-wax washer, elastic, wood lath.

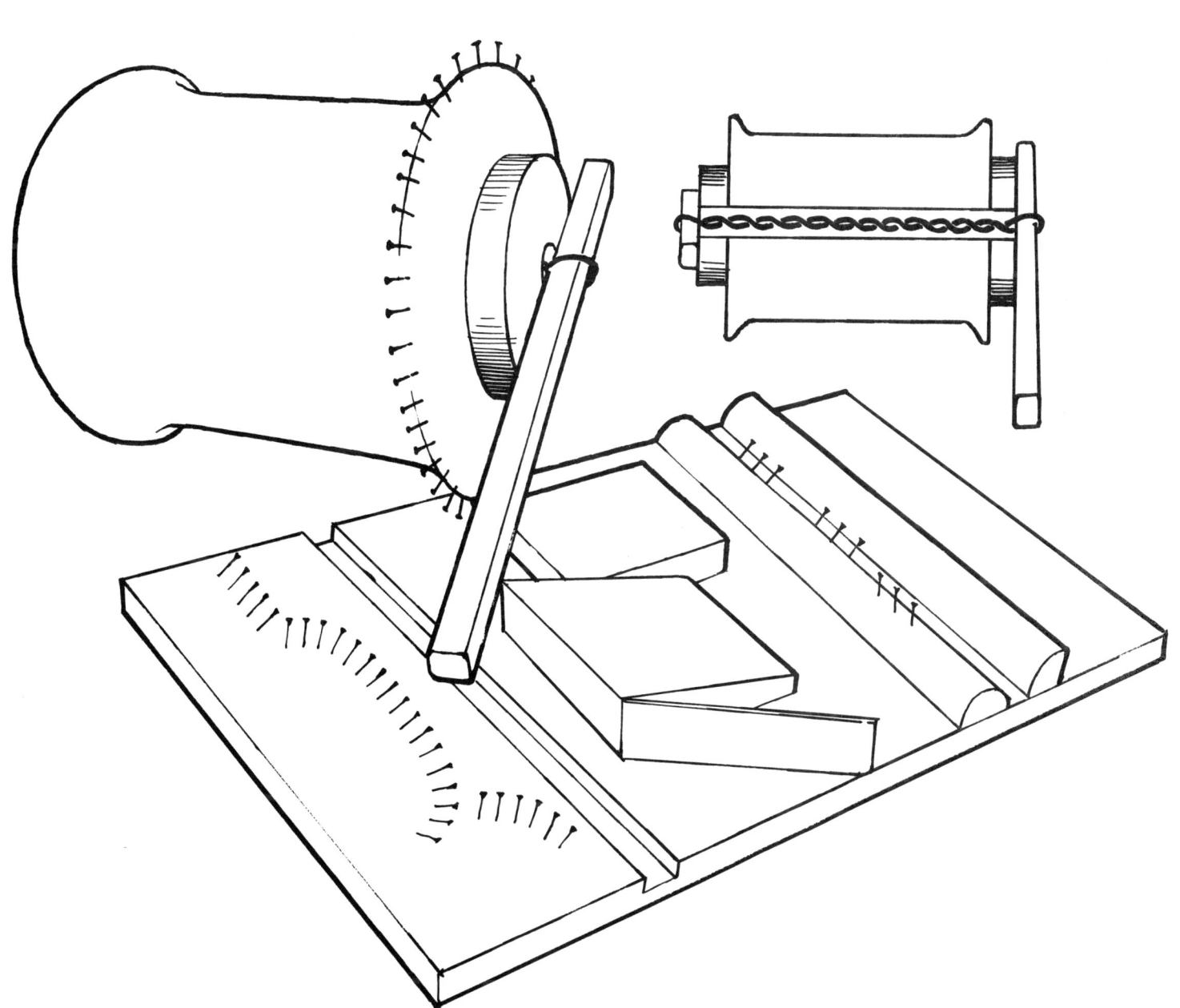

44
Skate Board

Solves the question of what to do with that one roller skate that always seems to be around. (Note that heel grips have to be flattened first.)
  Materials: old skate, pine board.

Whirlie Board

When all the beds in the school had their casters changed, I inherited 250 casters. They lay in a box for ages; then someone placed four on the corners of a board large enough to sit on to make a whirlie board. Great fun to be pushed and pulled around on.
  Materials: casters, board, plywood, etc.

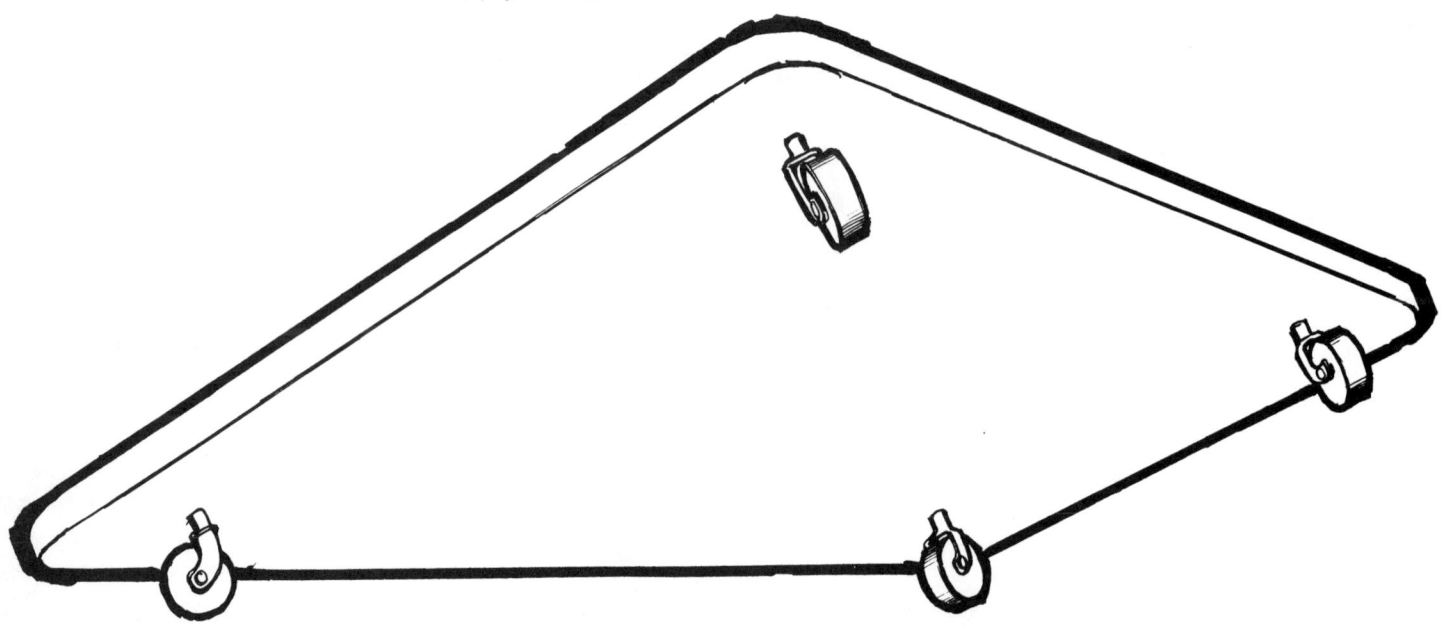

45
Stilts

Once you get the swing of how to walk on them, the height at which the feet blocks are positioned is determined by strength of material and nerve.

Money Box

A simple pine box. If required to be opened regularly, a screw bottom is advisable; otherwise glue and nail the whole thing (cut open to remove contents). A simple tinplate device prevents money being removed from the slot. Decoration by branding looks good.

46
Toilet-Roll Holder

I have made several for Summerhill and years later they are still going strong, whereas other types haven't made it. Curiously, when in order to make the holder strong I used a single dovetail joint, the children were inspired to use the joint on their boxes (and not to make roll holders).

Materials: dowel rod, pinewood or hardwood board.

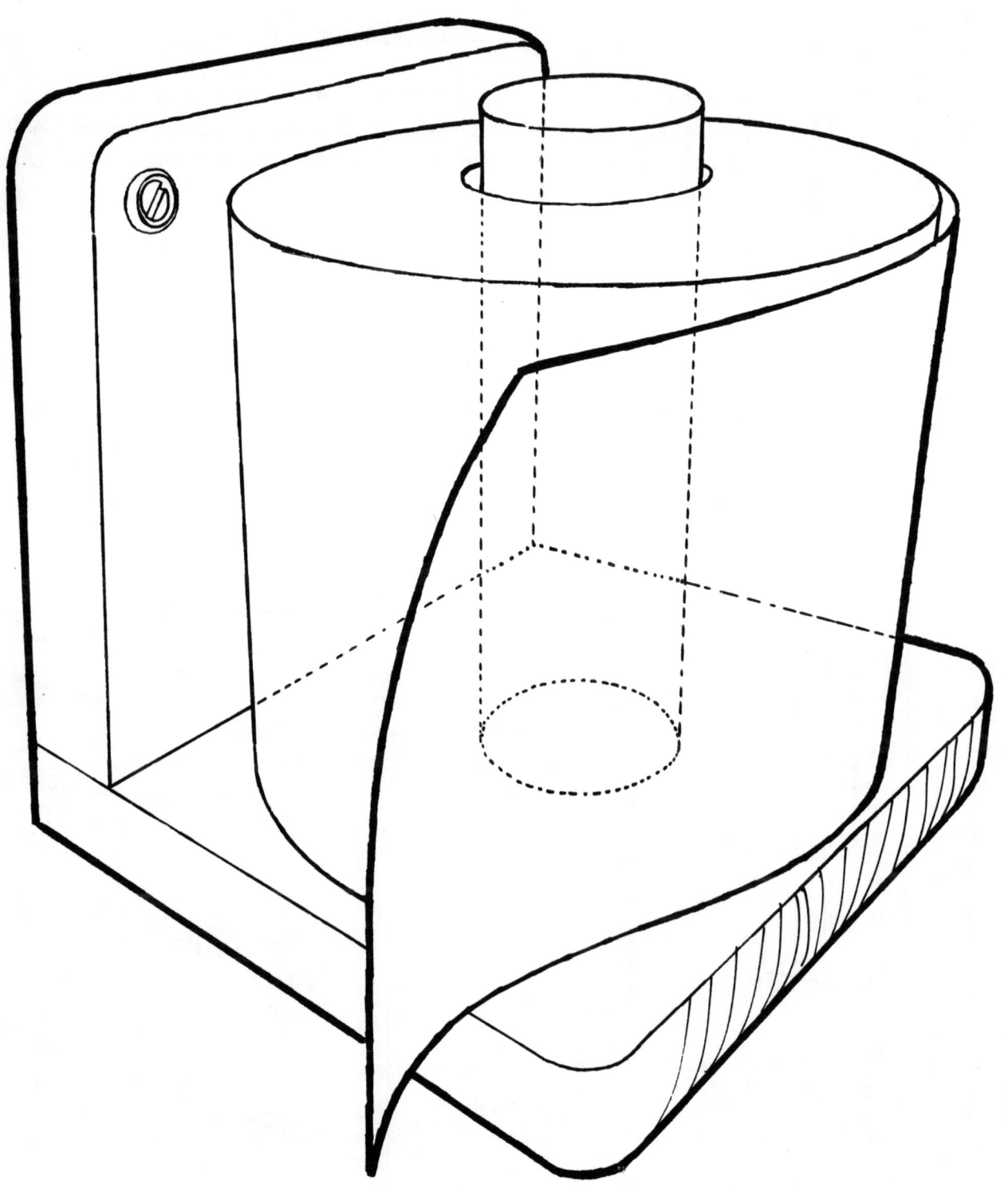

47
Tuck Box

This above all other things is what everyone in Summerhill has made at one time or another. It's a strongbox in which to keep odd things like cookies and chocolate that are liable to disappear if not removed from sight. The making of the box is simple: four sides and a top and bottom, hinged together, and a hasp and staple to take a lock. Refinements include a corner block on the inside, and the outside covered in tinplate, which looks good, to say the least.

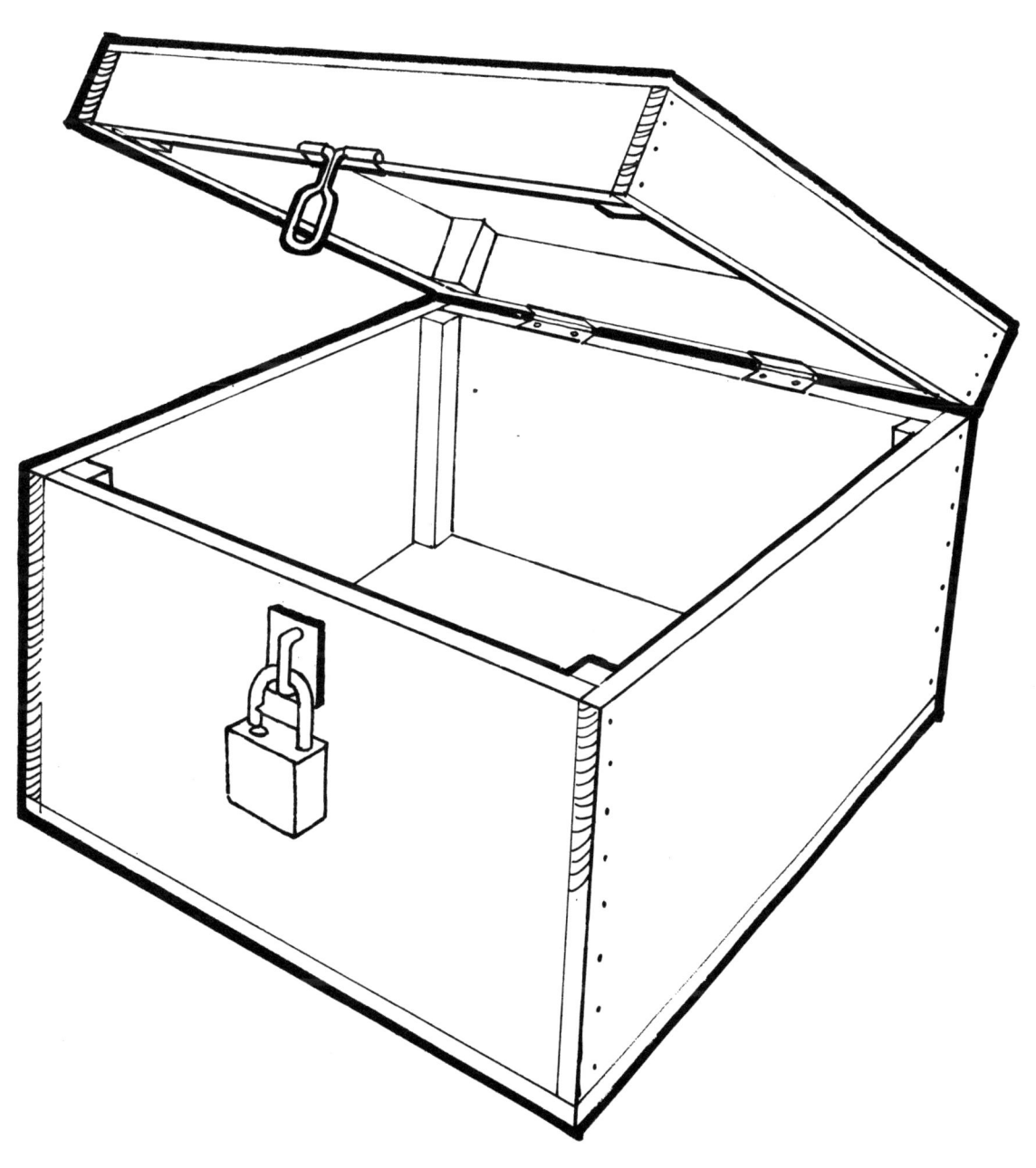

48
Letter Rack

Very easily made and very useful as well. Branding can be used for decoration as well as the printing. I have four on my desk: one to hold unused envelopes, the others for mail in and out and for letters in need of a reply.

Materials: softwood section and thin board.

Mousetrap

As the autumn gets under way, mice come in from the fields to winter in the house and outbuildings. Some of the children try to trap them by building humane mousetraps. The first one is simply a box with a drop door, operated by someone after the mouse has gone in. (This requires patience or an inventive mind to design a trip wire or something similar.) The other one is a bicycle tube down which the mouse goes to eat the bait; the mouse is unable to return up the tube because it collapses if he tries.

Materials: pine board, wire mesh, rubber tube.

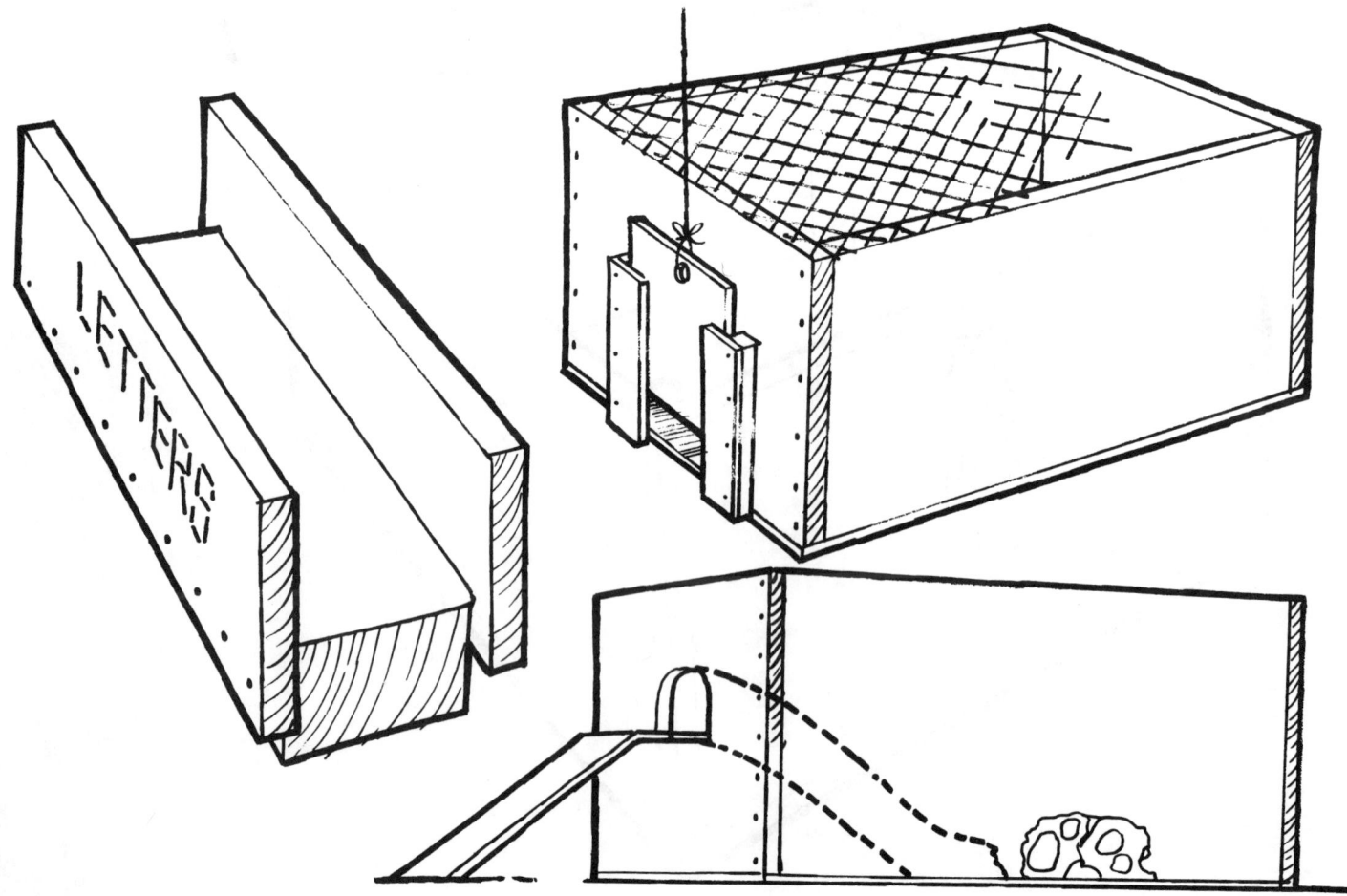

49
Picture Mounts

(a) The simplest way I've come across to mount pictures or photographs is as shown here, using clips made up from thin steel or copper stripping. Two clips per side hold the glass and print onto the backing board. (b) If a regular frame without glass is required, then a simple rectangle laid over the print and glued on a backboard works very well. If mitred joints aren't wanted, then simple butt joints work well using this method. (c) The double-rectangle frame is one rectangle outside the dimensions of the print or picture, with a covering rectangle glued to it. The glass, print, and backboard are held in by clips.

Materials: chipboard or plywood, pinewood or hardwood section, glass, clips.

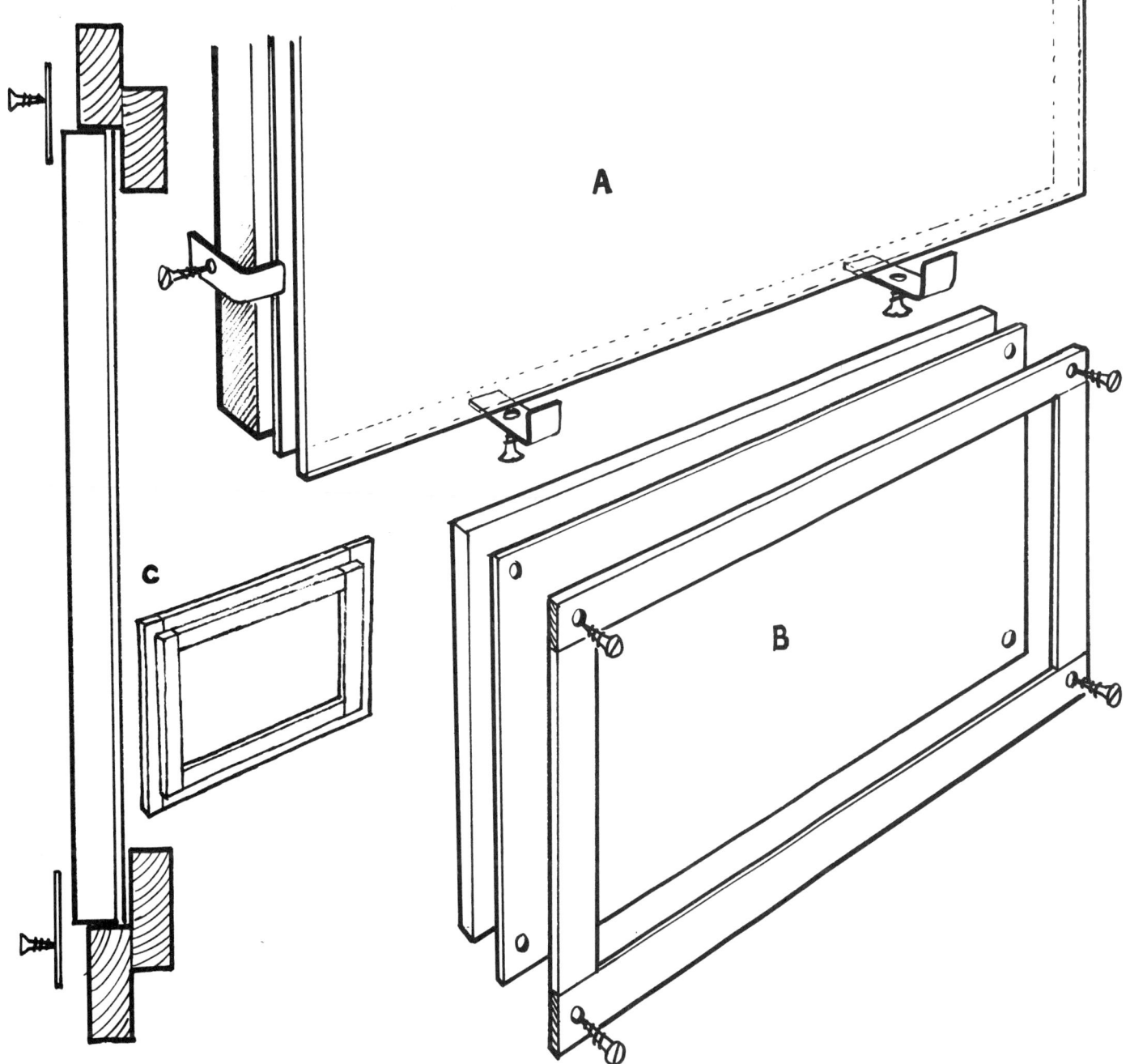

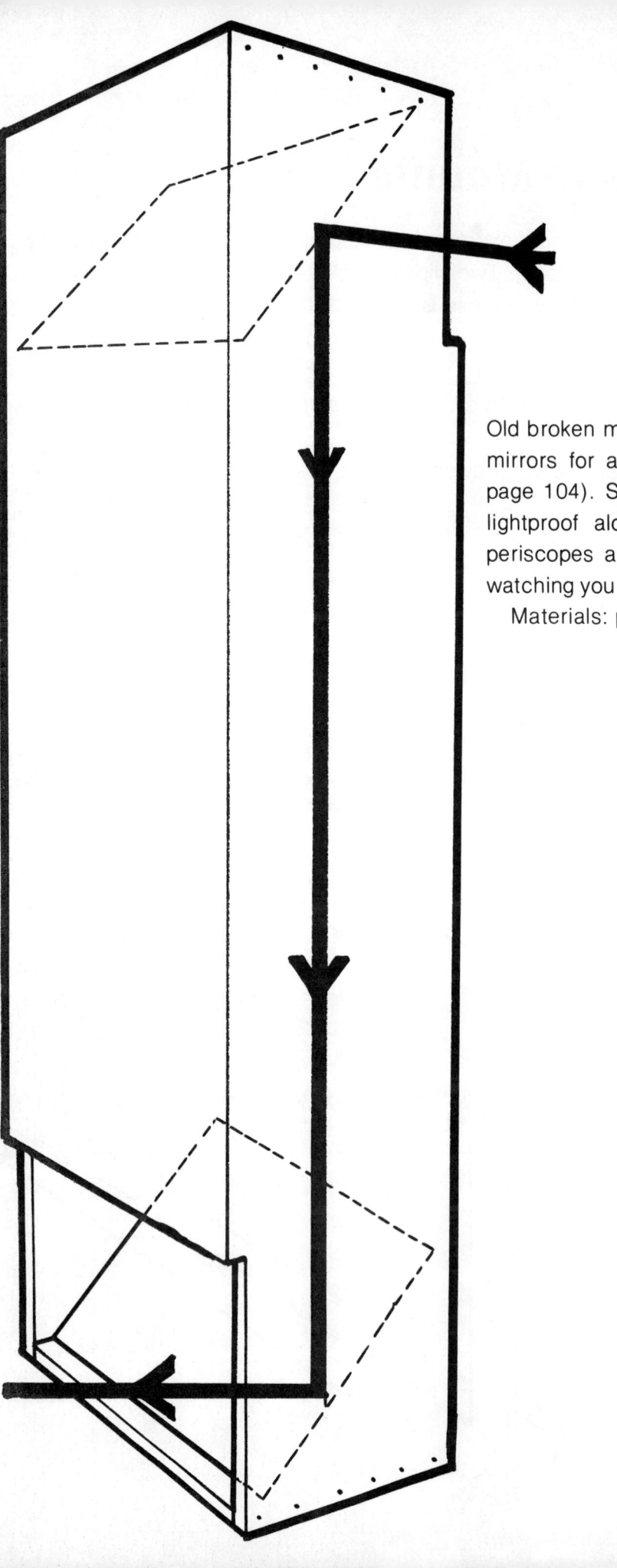

50
Periscope

Old broken mirrors can be trimmed to make a pair of mirrors for a periscope (see also mirror picture on page 104). Set the mirrors at 45°. The box must be lightproof along the joints for best results. When periscopes are about, you never quite know who is watching you or from where.

Materials: pine plank or plywood, two mirrors.

52
Woodware

Some of the things that can be made on a wood-turning lathe: candlestick, bowls, mugs and goblets, egg cups, table-lamp base, cookie barrel with lid, chair and stool legs, tops for glass jars, etc.

53
Tin-Can Ware

Tin cans and lids can be turned into many useful things. Cut a slot in a tin-can lid and solder it back onto the tin can and it's a money box. A tin-can lid can be made into a candle holder by soldering on wind guard and candle support. A camper's tin mug is made from a cut-down can with safety edge and handle added. The funnel is made from a tin can with a tube soldered at the hole made in the bottom. You can also make tin-can stilts with wooden handles, a megaphone, etc.

Materials: clean cans, etc.

54
Oil Lamps

Pipe tobacco tins with a tinplate tube soldered in the middle of the lid make good oil lamps. These were developed, along with various wind shields for the lamps, when the school was plunged into darkness during winter power strikes. Halloween lanterns, traditionally made from pumpkins, can be made from old cans, with punch holes for the face (it helps if the lid is still partially attached). The oil lamps can even be the light source, or else use candles.

Materials: clean tin cans and tins, string wick.

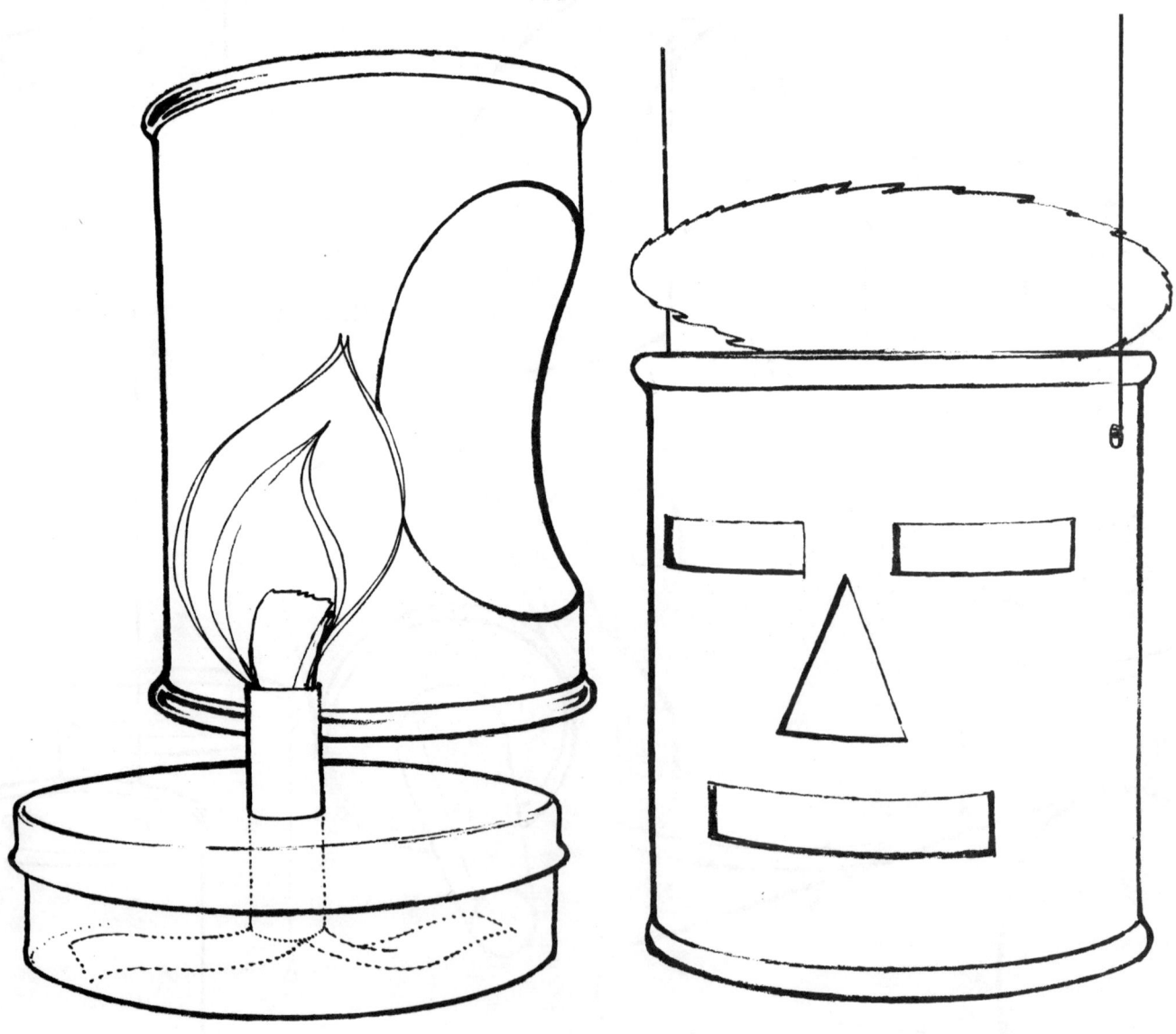

55
Lampshades

Large cans can be adapted for use as lampshades, but ventilation holes are a must, as more heat is developed from a light bulb than might at first be realized. Angle poise lamps are useful on a desk or bedside table. The combinations of how to make one work seem to be endless (and bring out the inventor in all of us).

Materials: tin cans, thin pine slats.

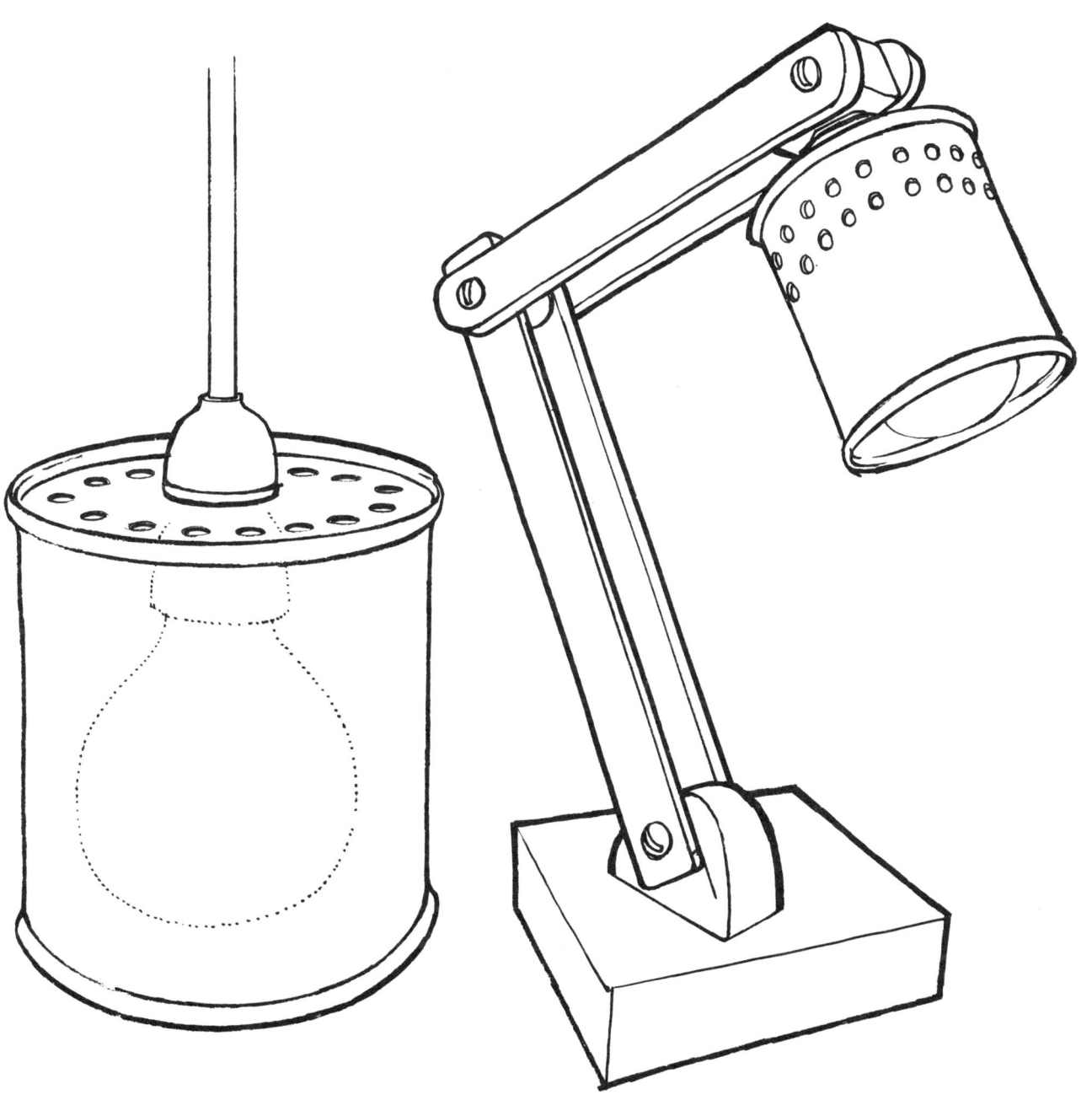

57
Basic Cart

These are made whenever wheels become available (cornering hard seems to reduce wheel life). Steering is conventional—string from an axle slung under the seat board. Back rests are optional extras.

Materials: board and wheels.

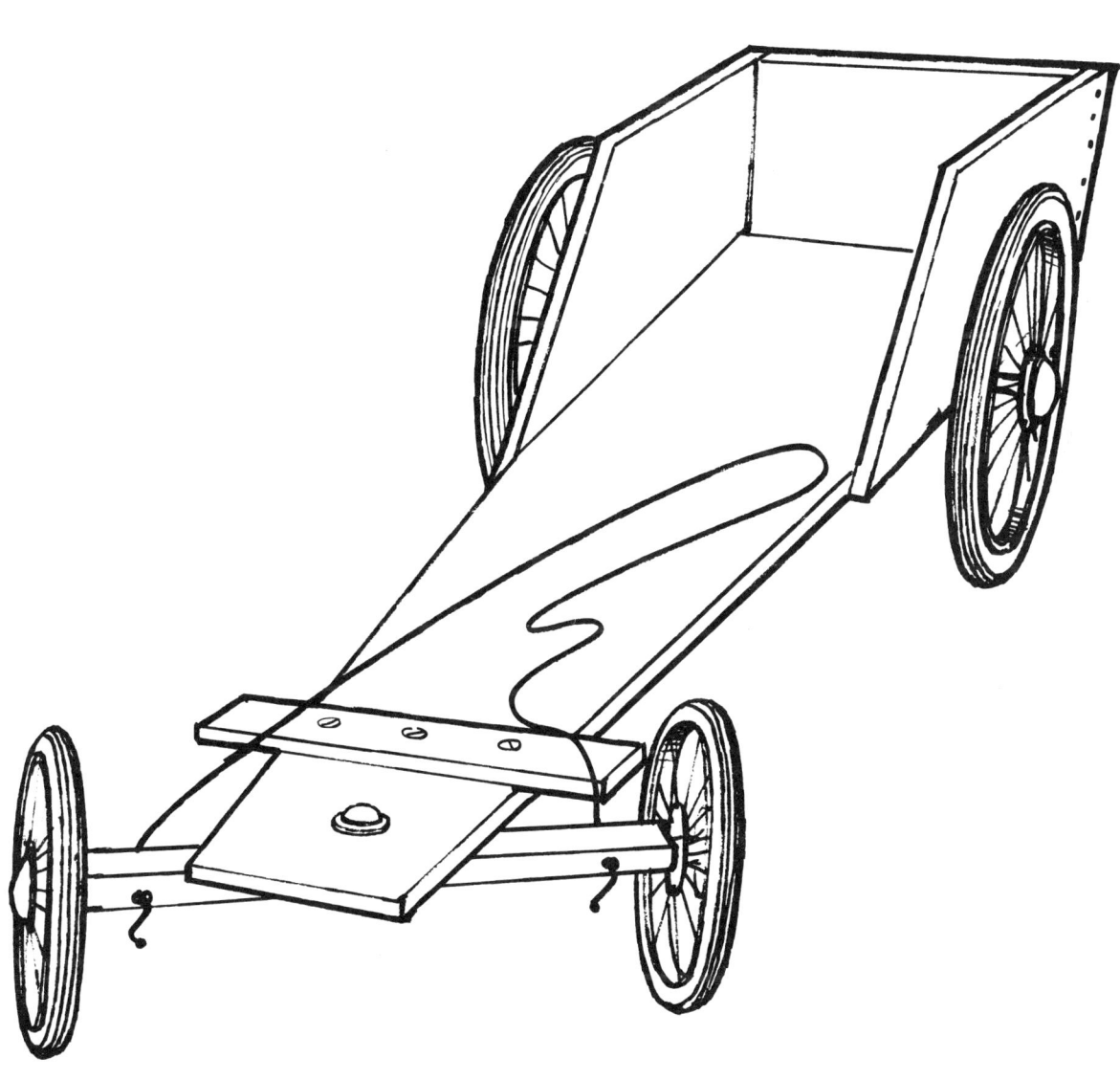

58
Tri Cart

The three-wheeled cart developed as a joke. Someone fitted the front-fork-wheel-handlebar combination of a small bicycle into a thick board and had cartwheels on the back. It was so successful, especially when towed around the school behind a cycle, that several were made. The ultimate of these machines even had rear suspension.

Materials: boards, wheel combinations.

60
Model Cannons

Model cannons are very popular and quite easily turned on the metal lathe. It's good to have authentic pictures to work from, but not essential; the end products all seem to look good. Blacking the barrel by heating it to dull red heat and then immersing it in dirty oil is always very popular because it's dramatic and causes clouds of dense smoke.

Materials: aluminum, mild steel, brass, wood fittings.

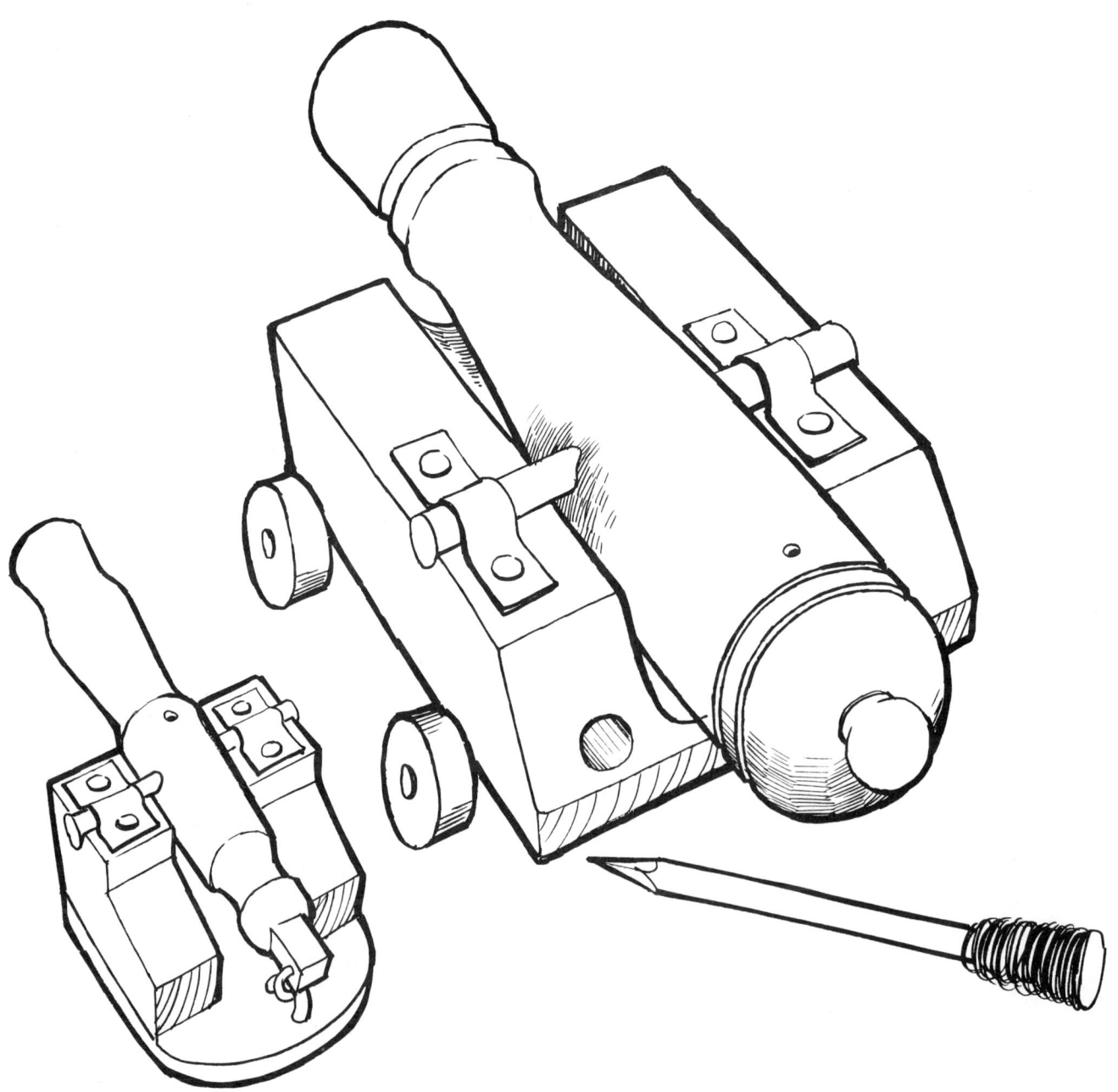

61
Metal Cast

A tray filled with damp sand and smoothed makes rough casting of house numbers and other simple shapes fairly easy. Casting becomes more technical when complicated shapes have to be cast, so on the whole we keep it simple. We once had a cast of someone's face done this way. Interesting work can be done even though it's on a simple level.

62
Belts and Buckles

I think in the space of two terms everyone in the school made a belt, and being as each one is good for a few years, if not a lifetime, repeat orders have been few. Buckles are easily made, especially out of brass. The cross bar and catch are soldered on afterwards. I bought some very fine harness buckles from the local saddler, which proved popular. Brass eyelets look smart for the belt holes. If tooling is to be done on the belt, experiment on scraps beforehand.

   Materials: brass in sheet and rod, split or cap rivets.

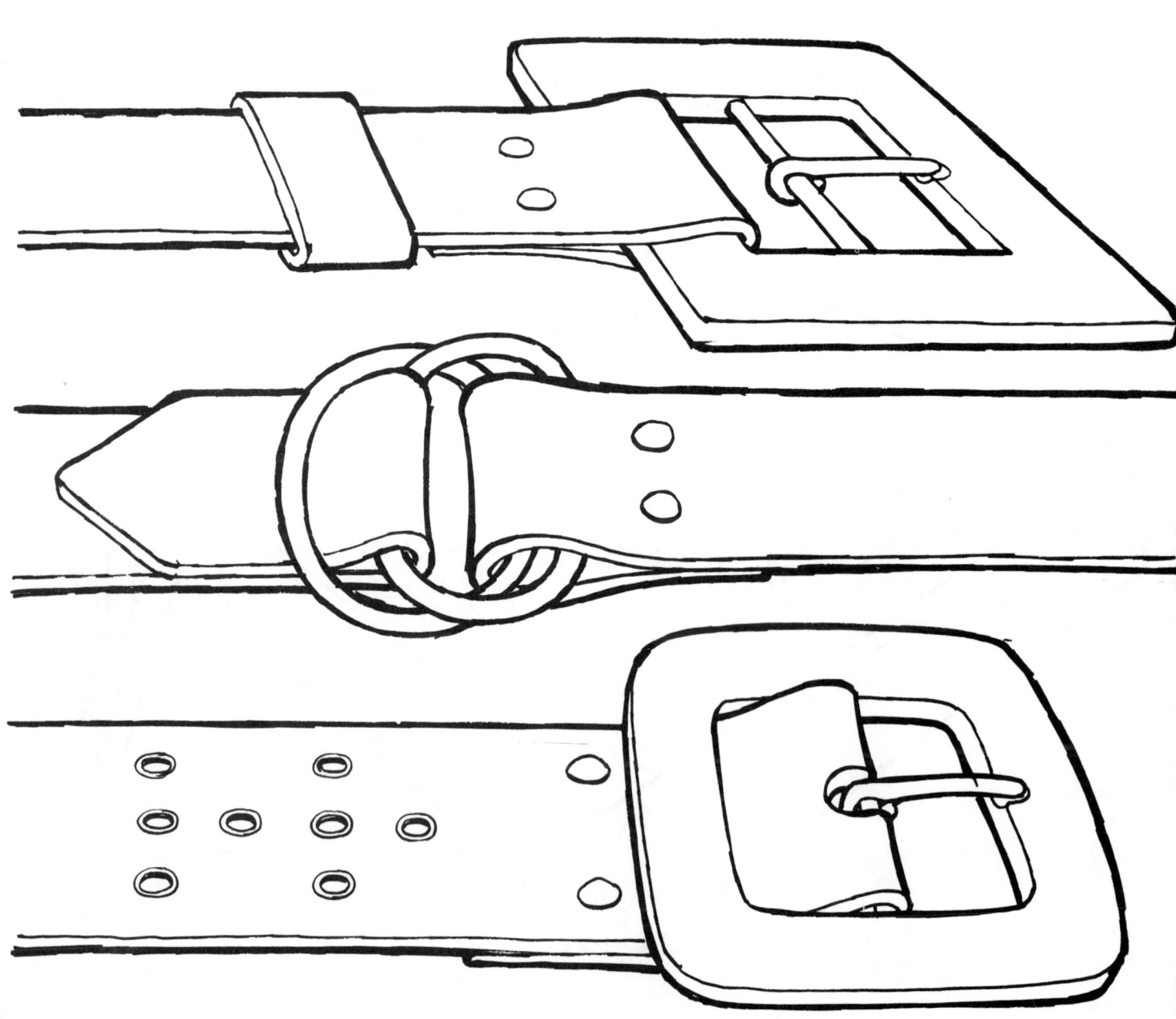

63
Sandals and Flip-Flops

During the summer term many pairs of leather sandals and flip-flops are made. It is best to use an existing pair as a pattern and then adapt that if necessary. The layers of the sandal are glued together with impact adhesive. Middle layers have to have cut-outs to accommodate where the straps are riveted to the top layer, otherwise uncomfortable bumps are there. Short brass tacks around the edge give a finishing touch and help keep the whole shoe secure.

Materials: sheet leather, impact glue, split or cap rivets, brass tacks.

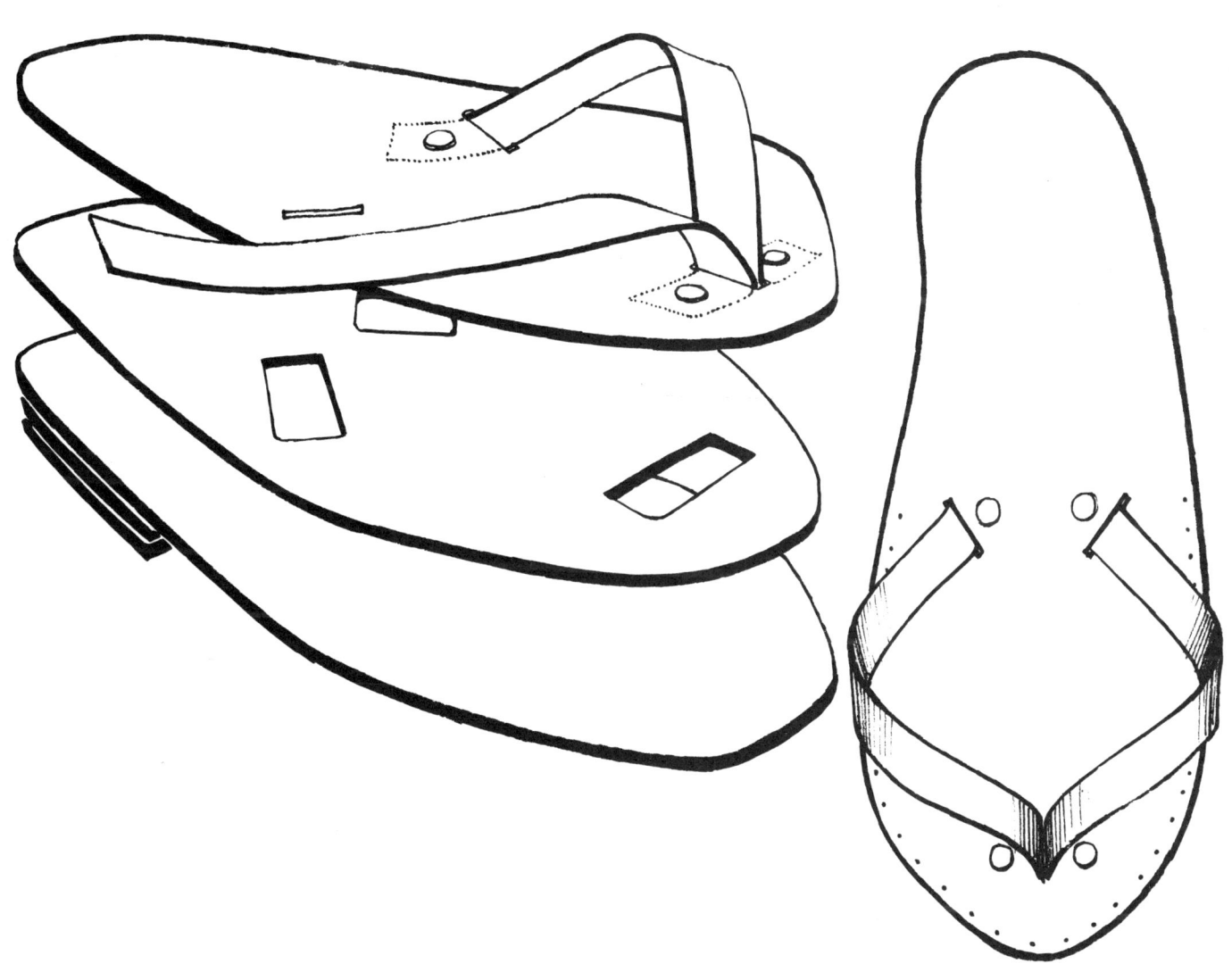

64
Mobile

Mobiles are an interesting project and can incorporate a wide range of materials from wood scraps through plastics to enamels. The end balance-pieces can be made into pendants when the mobile is dismantled.

Materials: wire, plastics, wood, metals, dowel rods.

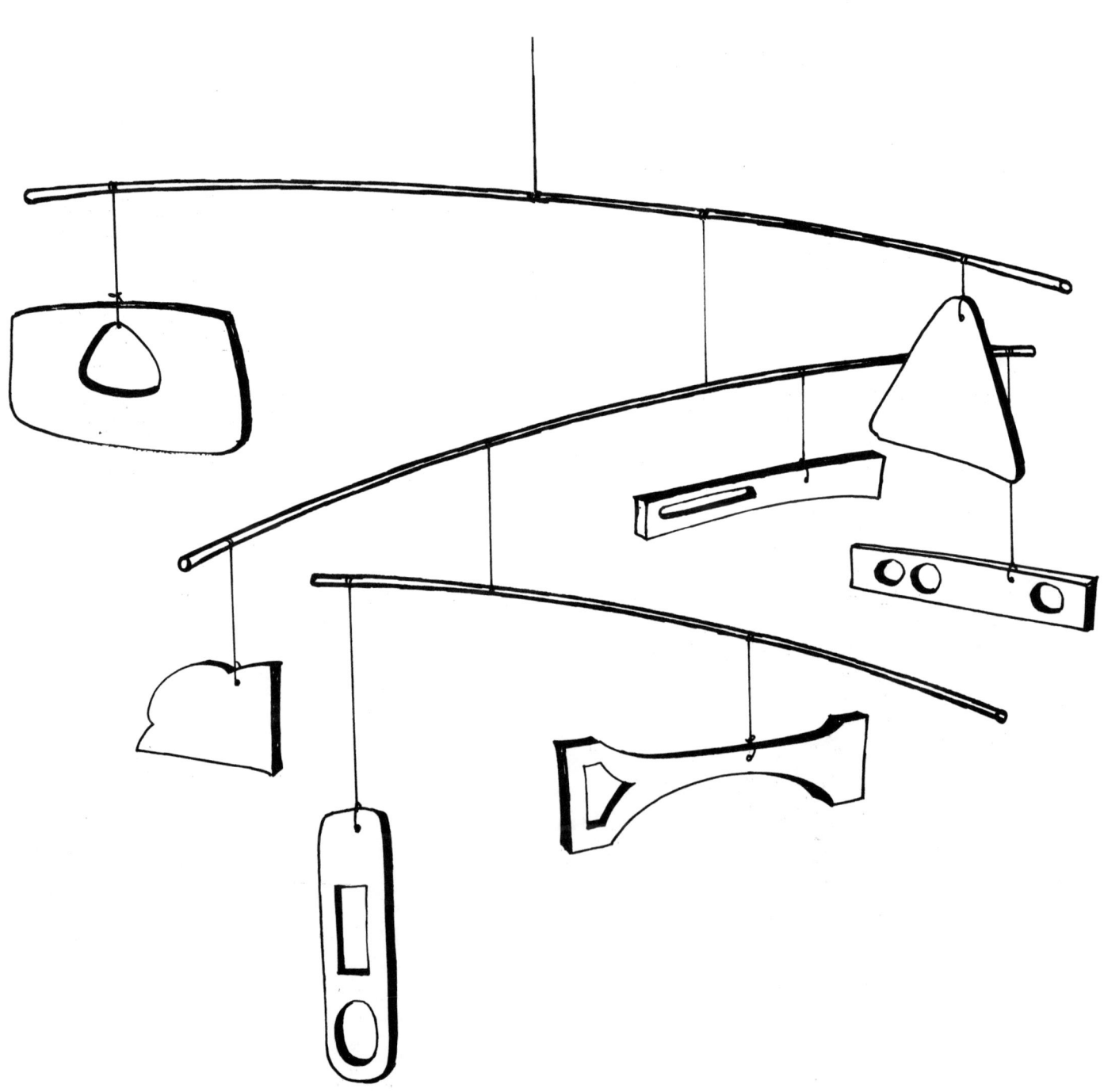

65
Jewelry

Obviously a great deal could be said about jewelry. All I want to mention are the main items that have been made in Summerhill—rings, pendants, and earrings. We work mostly in silver during special lessons and in copper with the younger children.

(1) Plain silver rings are what the children usually start with. The rings don't have to be round—I've seen some very nice ones that are rounded squares and triangles.

(2) Plaited or twisted wires of different section can be hammered flat to make interesting rings.

(3) Laminated rings are quite interesting. I made a whole series once combining silver and ebony, a very pleasing combination. Plastics and metals can be very effective, and unusual shaped rings lend themselves to laminates.

(4) Stone setting isn't as difficult as it might at first seem. However, it is best to become proficient at soldering before starting an ambitious project.

(5) Earrings are always popular. Simple drop earrings can be made without much experience. Tubed silver, cut up and soldered at random, looks most interesting. Bezel-set stones require a little more expertise.

(6) Pendants and necklaces are fairly straightforward. The fashion at the moment is to have neck wires or collars instead of chains.

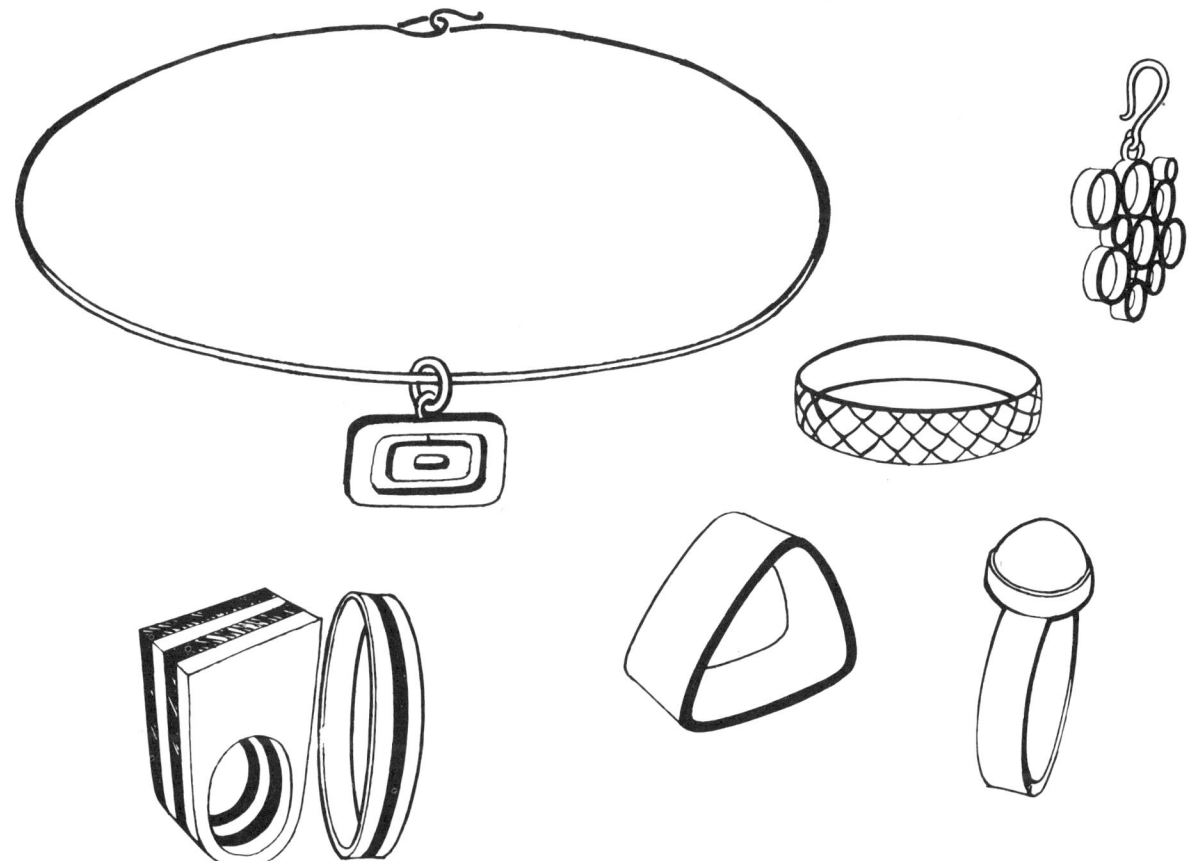

66
Circular Stool

Circular stools that are light and very strong can be made from two discs of plywood, spaced with pine rods, and wrapped around on the outside with a thin skin of plywood. A cushion on the top is held in place by protruding lips. The corner made by the lip and top can be filleted with a resin filler, as can be the depression where the outside skin edges meet.

Materials: plywoods and pinewoood section, resin filler.

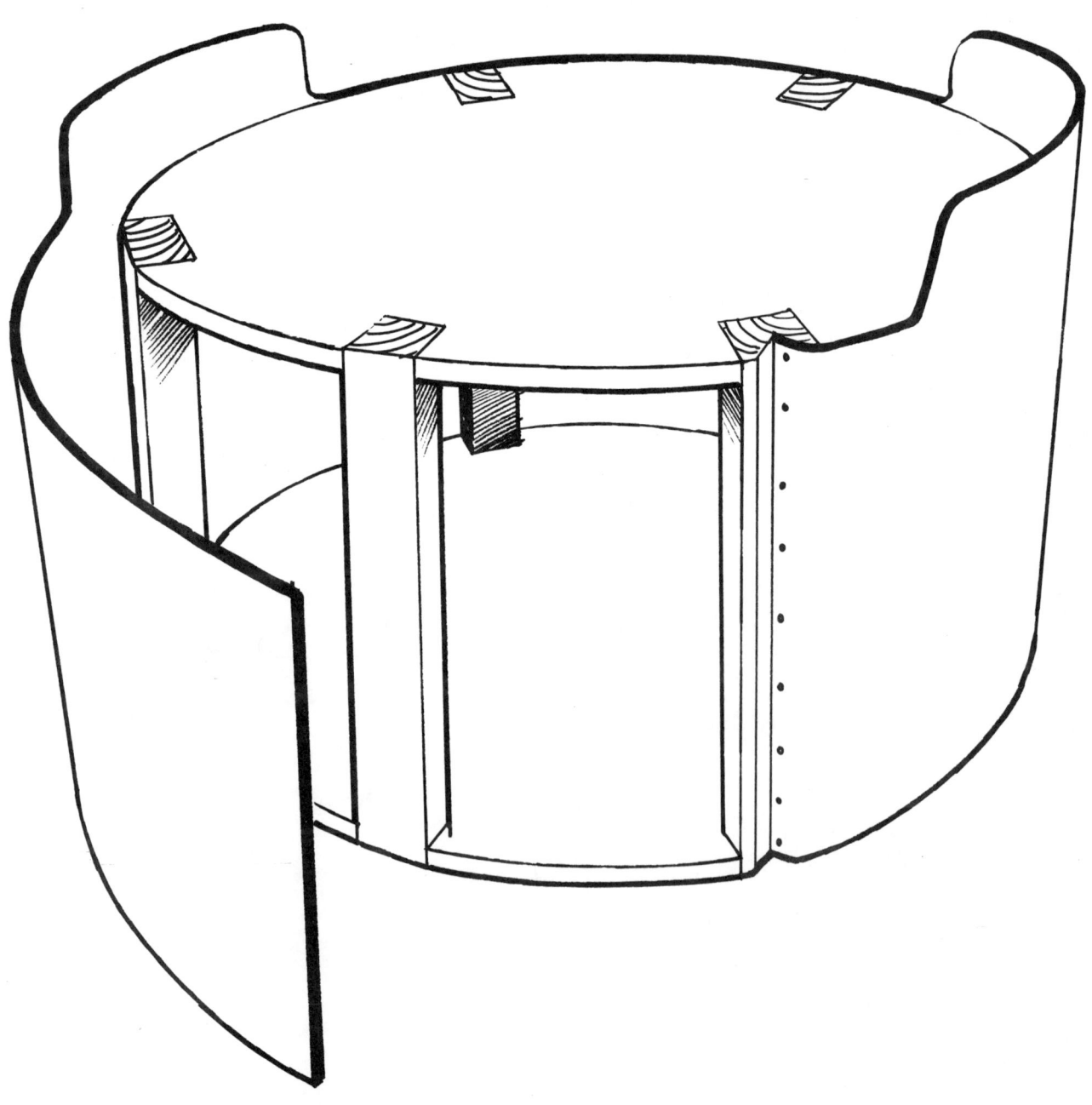

67
Three-Legged Stool

A circular top turned on the lathe and three legs, either dowel rod or also turned on the lathe. Legs are tapered into holes in the top and wedged so as to form a strong joint.

Materials: hardwoods or softwoods, dowel rods.

End-Frame Stool

A pair of frames (various shapes) with a middle rectangle between them makes a good stool and dispenses with complicated joints that seem to prevail in stool construction. Seat can be either a cushion or upholstered.

Materials: hardwood or softwood section, plywood seat.

68
Laminates

Salad servers can be made from laminating veneers. A simple mold is made from a large section of timber cut through to the shape required. Strips of veneer, freshly glued, are placed within the cut, and the whole block is held in a vice or with clamps. With more complicated shapes for, say, chairs or stools, the veneer is more manageable if it has been soaked in water previously and is allowed to dry in its clamped position.

Materials: laminated wood or veneer, large section timber.

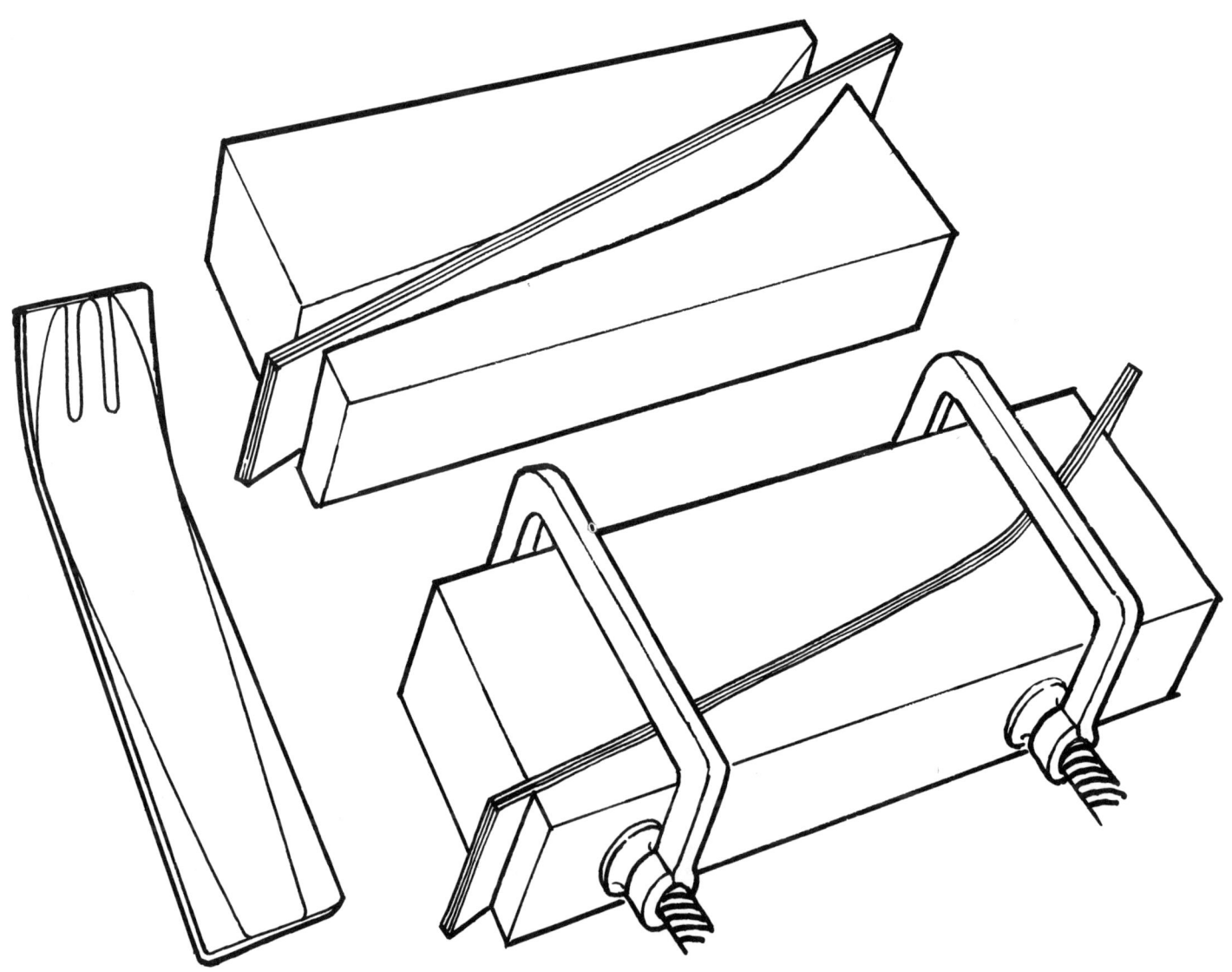

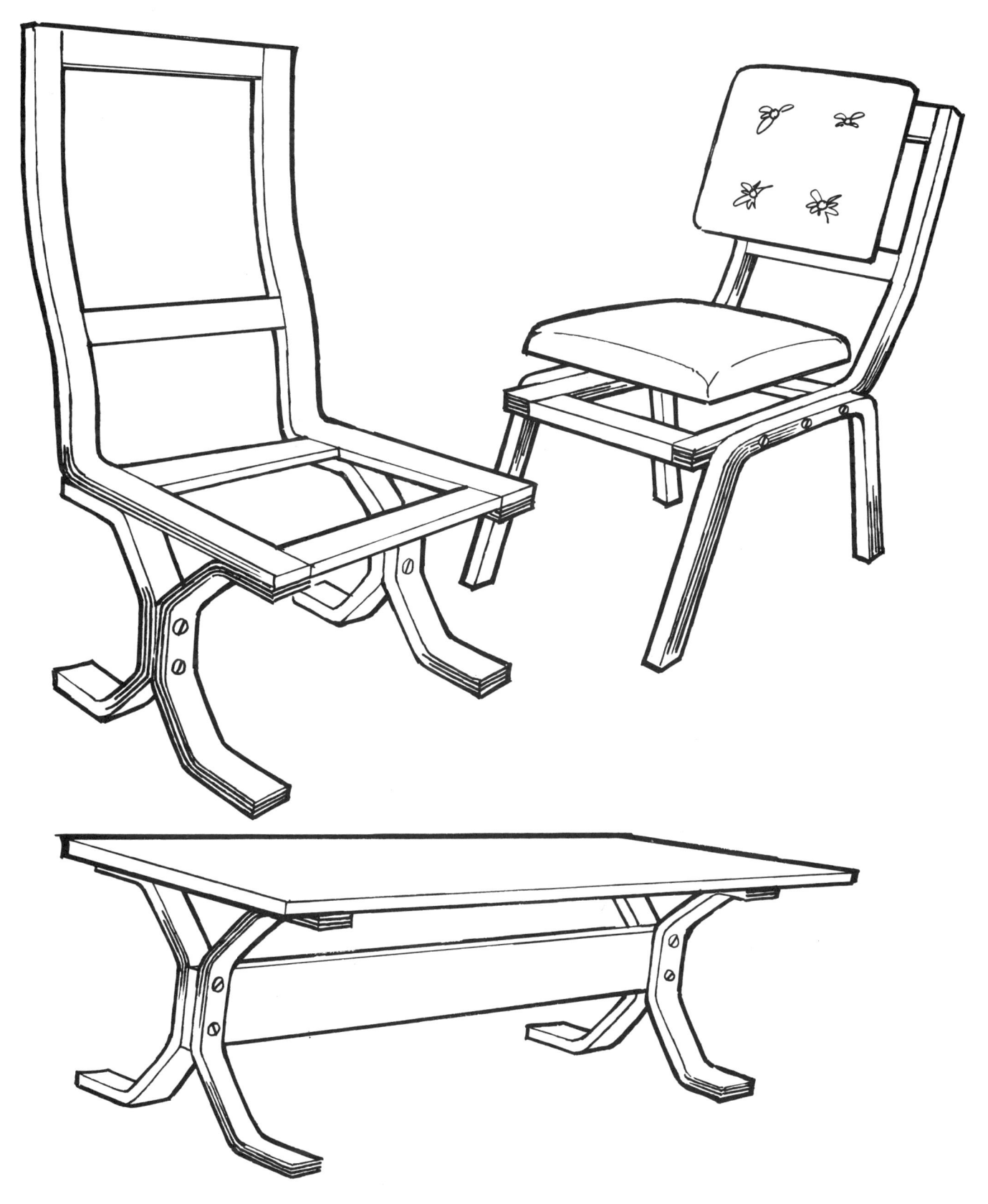

70
Car Seats

Seats and settees have a fairly high death rate in schools, so whenever possible the children get hold of old car seats and make them usable. Bench-type seats tend to fall over backwards rather easily so it's necessary to have a couple of pieces of wood or angle iron sticking out a foot or so at the back. For the more ambitious, a frame can easily be welded together and put onto the underframe of the seats. Great for hideouts and TV rooms.

Materials: car seats, etc.

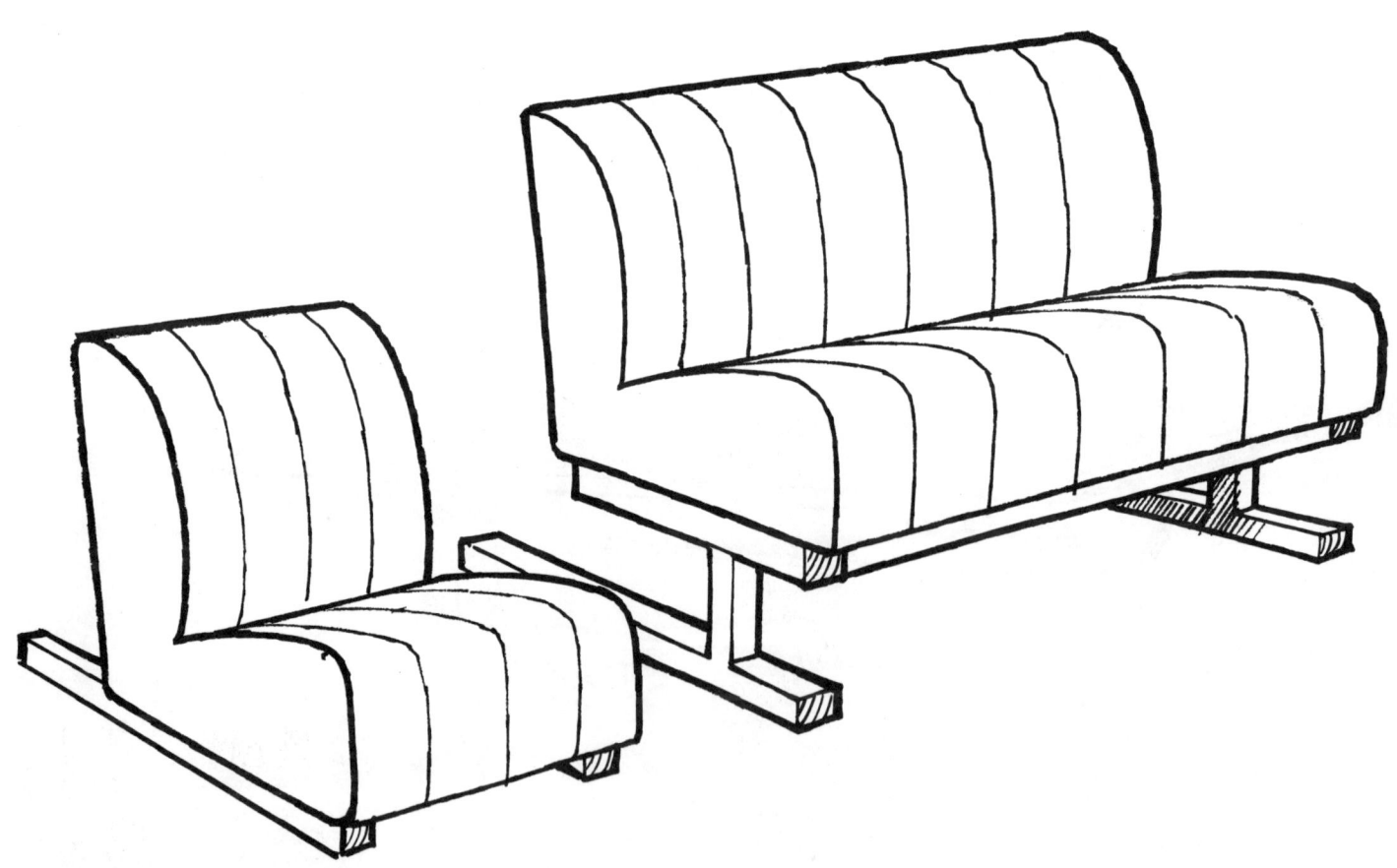

72
Bottle Cracking

This is a very old party trick used by the Victorians and a delight to children. A wine bottle is half filled with oil, a poker or metal bar heated to bright red heat is placed slowly through the neck and into the oil. The bottle 'pings' and cracks cleanly just above the oil line. When the oil has been drained off, the glass can be ground smooth on an oilstone.

I was a little dubious about this working, so tried it as an experiment—with success. Since then the children have made hundreds of drinking glasses, wind chimes, ash trays, etc.

The wind chimes are worthy of special note. The cracked-off bottle tops can be strung on a piece of twine using washers to space them out; a piece of board is tied on the end to catch the wind; then the chimes are hung on a branch and . . . They make a delightful tinkling sound. Not recommended in strong winds, however.

Materials: bottles, oil, iron rod.

74
Kite Reels and Kites

I'm pleased when someone decides to make a kite, as I really enjoy going out and flying one. Light dowel rods are lashed together in a cross and glued at the joint. Cover outside with old sheet, paper, plastic, etc. Stringing (determination of tail length, etc.) should be done on site for best performance. It's interesting to send kites up in tandem. Get one flying and then attach another to the line and get that up as well. It looks really fine. Reels are varied and can be made as desired.

   Materials: dowel rod, string, paper, plastic, or sheet.

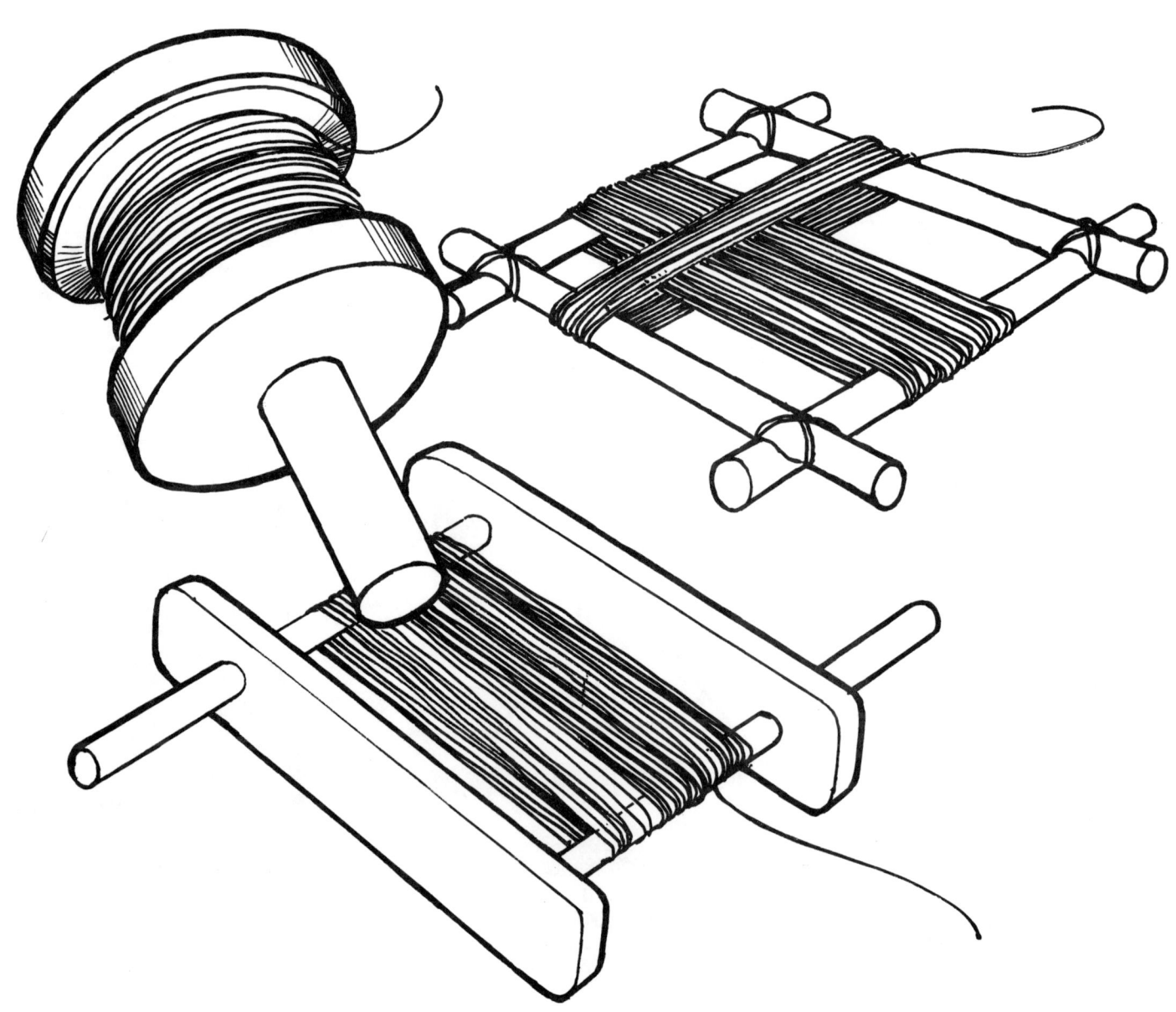

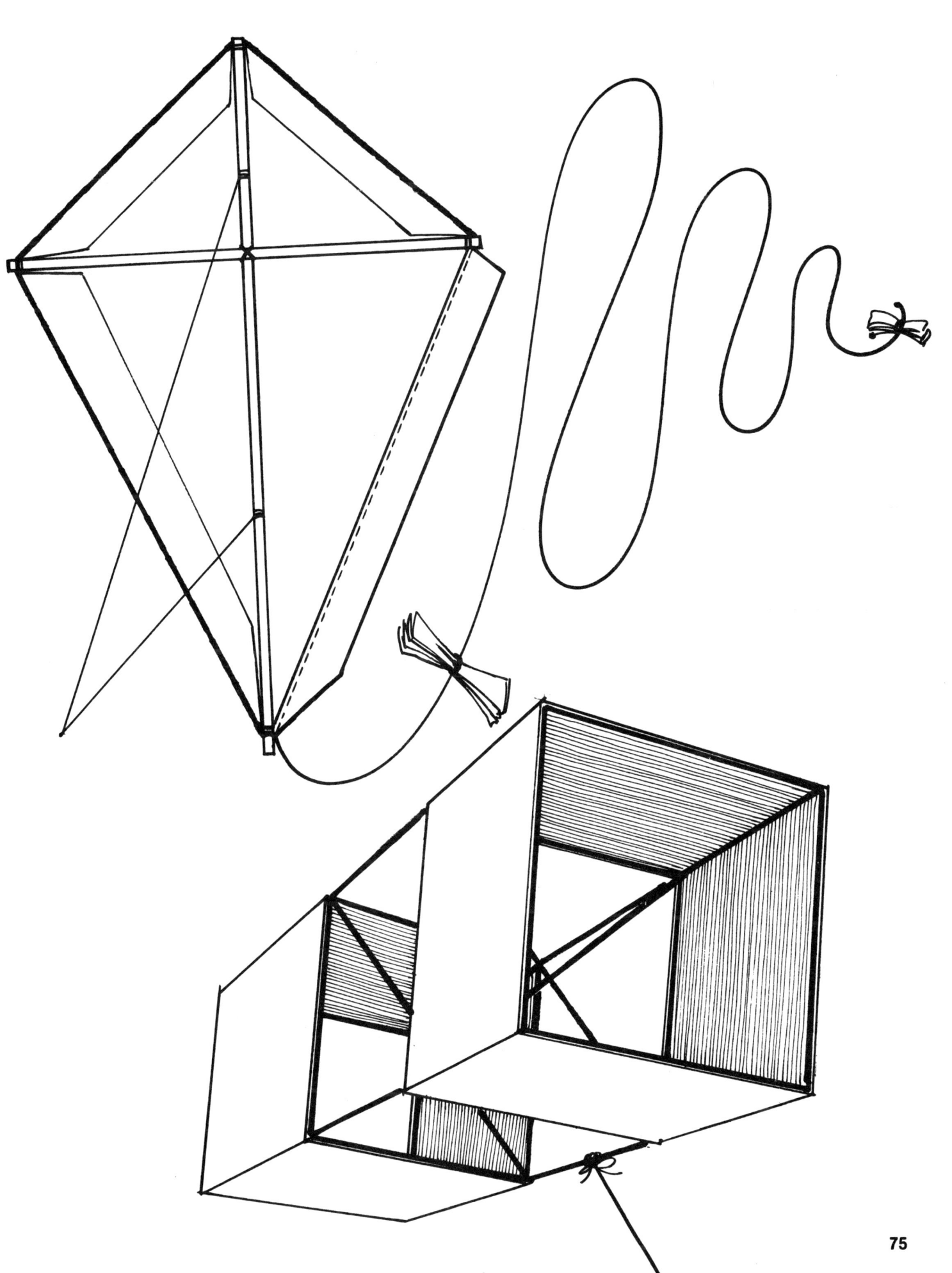

76
Conker Snake

Made seasonally when conkers (horse chestnuts) or acorns are about. The conkers are strung in order of size. Carved wood blocks are used for the snake's head and tail. Similar snakes can be made from dowel rod or blocks of wood strung together.
   Materials: string, scrap wood, conkers, acorns, etc.

Name Tag

These seem to be made when there is a new dog at home, or for some similar reason. If the children have difficulty keeping their letters straight, I suggest they make a feature of slanting letters.
   Materials: brass, copper, aluminum.

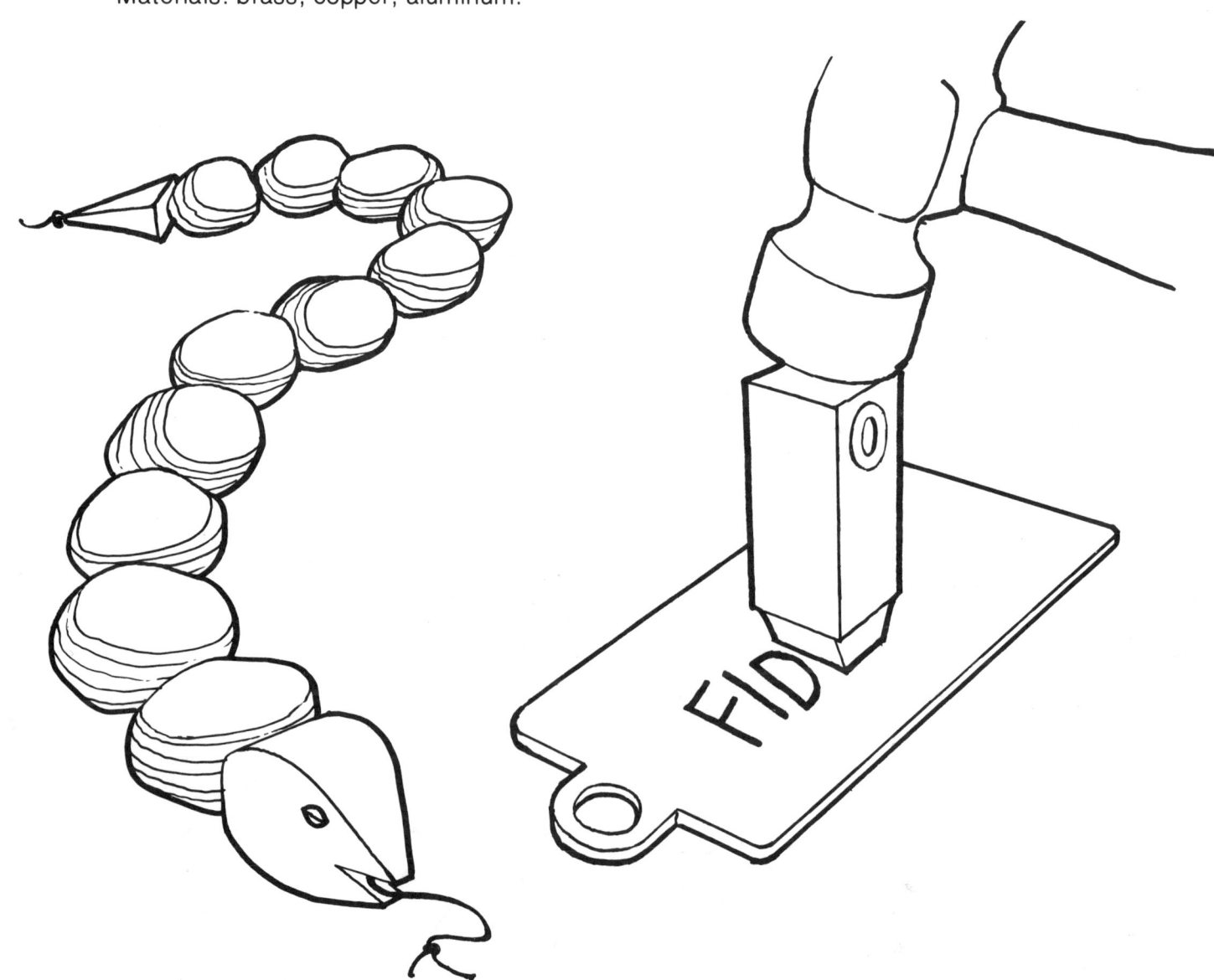

77
Robot

Robots usually get made from pieces of scrap wood and odd bits of wire around the workshop. Wheeled robots seem to overcome the mobility problems best. Branding can give a more technical look; some robots even get armor-plated.

Materials: scrap wood, wire, etc.

Walkie-Talkie

Make-believe walkie-talkies are very popular with our younger children. They vary in shape from the secret-service model, which can be very small and almost any shape, to the regular ones with telescopic car aerials and lots of impressive knobs.

Materials: scraps of wood, knobs, dowel rods, etc.

Tin-Can Walkie-Talkie

Strictly limited range. The end of each can acts as a diaphragm when the string or wire is stretched between the two cans.

Materials: two tin cans, string or thin wire.

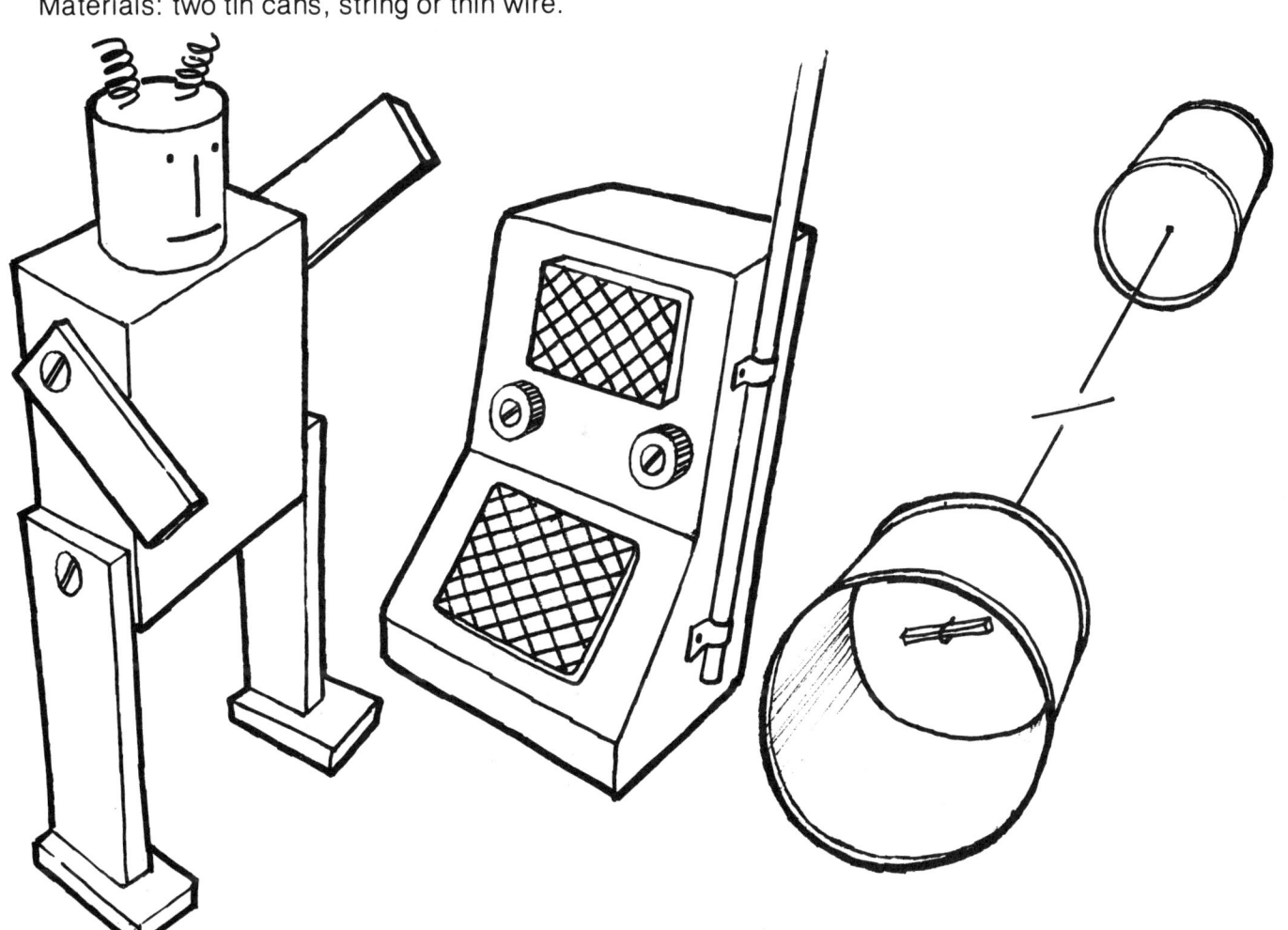

78
Wheels

A hole cutter with varying diameter blades is used in the workshop to make wheels for model cars, tanks, trains, or other vehicles, as well as to cut holes. Sections of bicycle inner tubes make good tires.

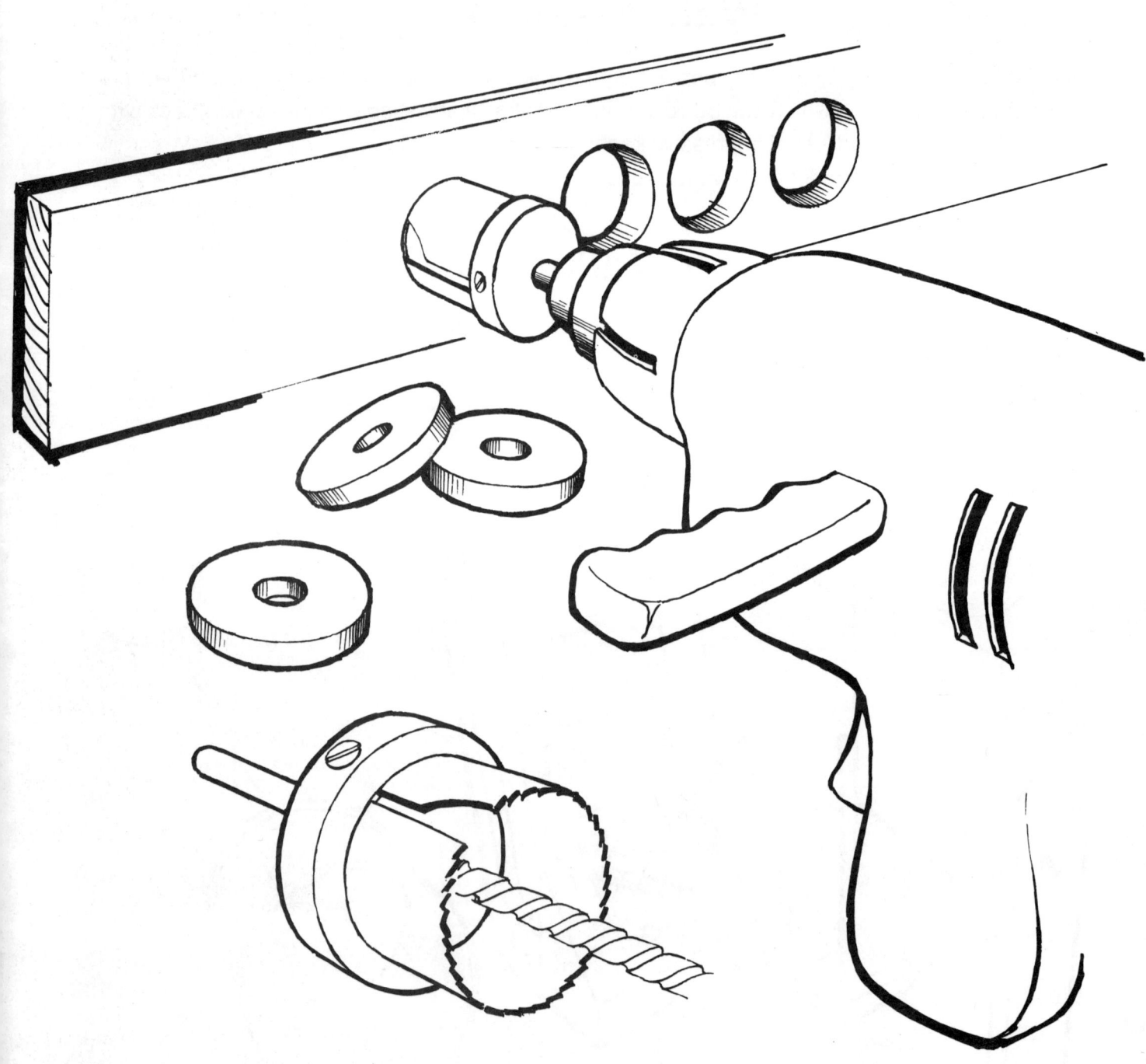

80
Dollhouse

Can be built from large cardboard boxes with one side made to swing open for access and building inside floors. Model beds, tables, and other pieces of furniture are made from odd pieces of wood and dowel rod.

The children seem to like the idea of using up all sorts of scraps and their inventiveness is amazing. We had one boy in Summerhill who, whenever there was a fashion for making something, would always make his own miniature version.

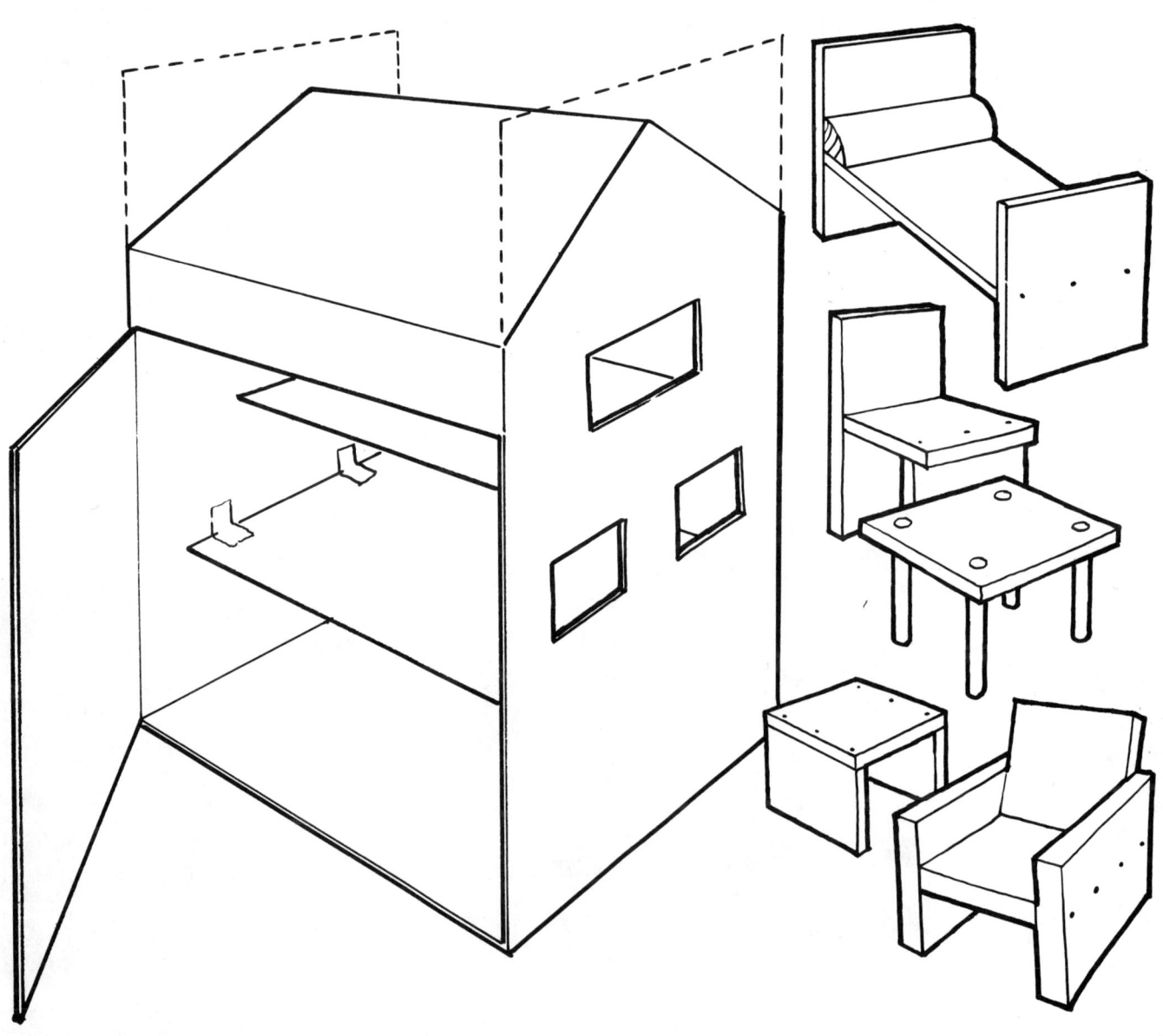

82
Badges

Everyone makes badges in Summerhill, especially for party games and special events like half term. The message, slogan, or picture is written on a piece of card and a safety pin is taped to the back of the card. Some days are declared smile days and so smile badges are worn. On sports day in the summer term everyone ends up with a badge of some sort; it seems much better and healthier than giving prizes, which seem to make the winning more important than being in the event.

  Materials: colored card, safety pins, tape.

Pipe Rack

The piece of wood used to make the four wheels for a model car can be used here for dad's pipe rack.

  Material: hardwood.

Pencil Holder

A must in every home. The children love drilling all the holes and then decorating the block with branded patterns or someone's name.

  Materials: softwood block.

83
Cages

Summer cages lie on the ground so that the rabbit or guinea pig can emerge from the living quarters and graze at will. These are made from rough-sawn pine and hardboard covered with chicken wire and creosoted for protection against the elements. The roof is made from chipboard covered with a plastic sack and is hinged to the main cage.

The winter cage is more of a draft excluder, being elevated and covered in on all but part of the front side. The construction is simple. The cage's strength is in the hardboard sides, which hold it all rigid.

On both cages the roof is covered with plastic sacks to keep the rain from soaking into the chipboard.

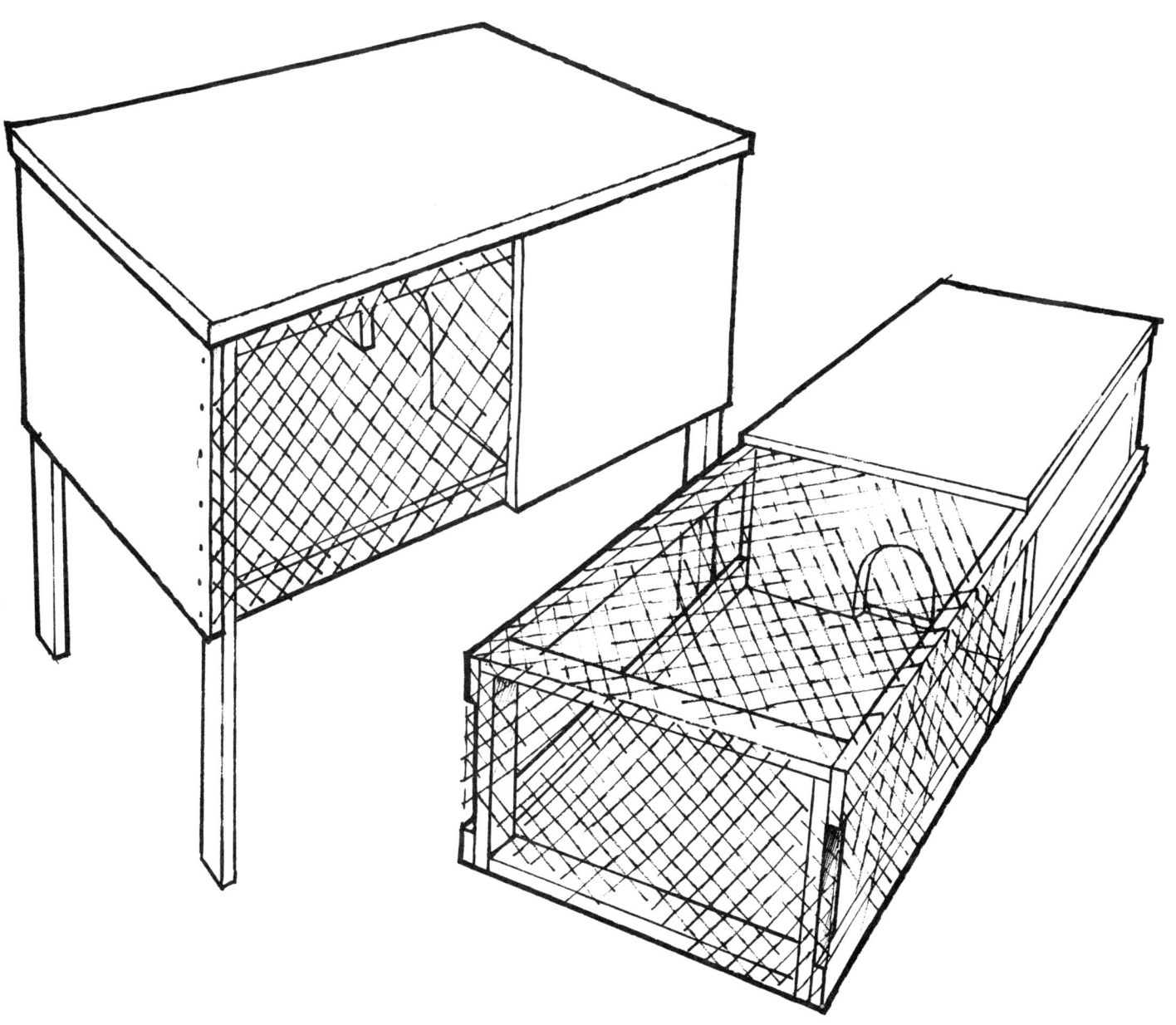

Scrap-Wood Box

The scrap-wood box is in a constant state of flux. Projects can be suggested using material from it as a base, e.g., build a model bridge or tower using pieces from out of the scrap box, then see whose model can take the most weight before it becomes unsafe. The scrap box is a whole book in itself—what one child throws away is another child's inspiration.

85
Towel Racks

Useful for the kitchen or bathroom. End pieces may be any shape and can be adapted for use of a roller towel.

Materials: pine board, laths, dowel rod.

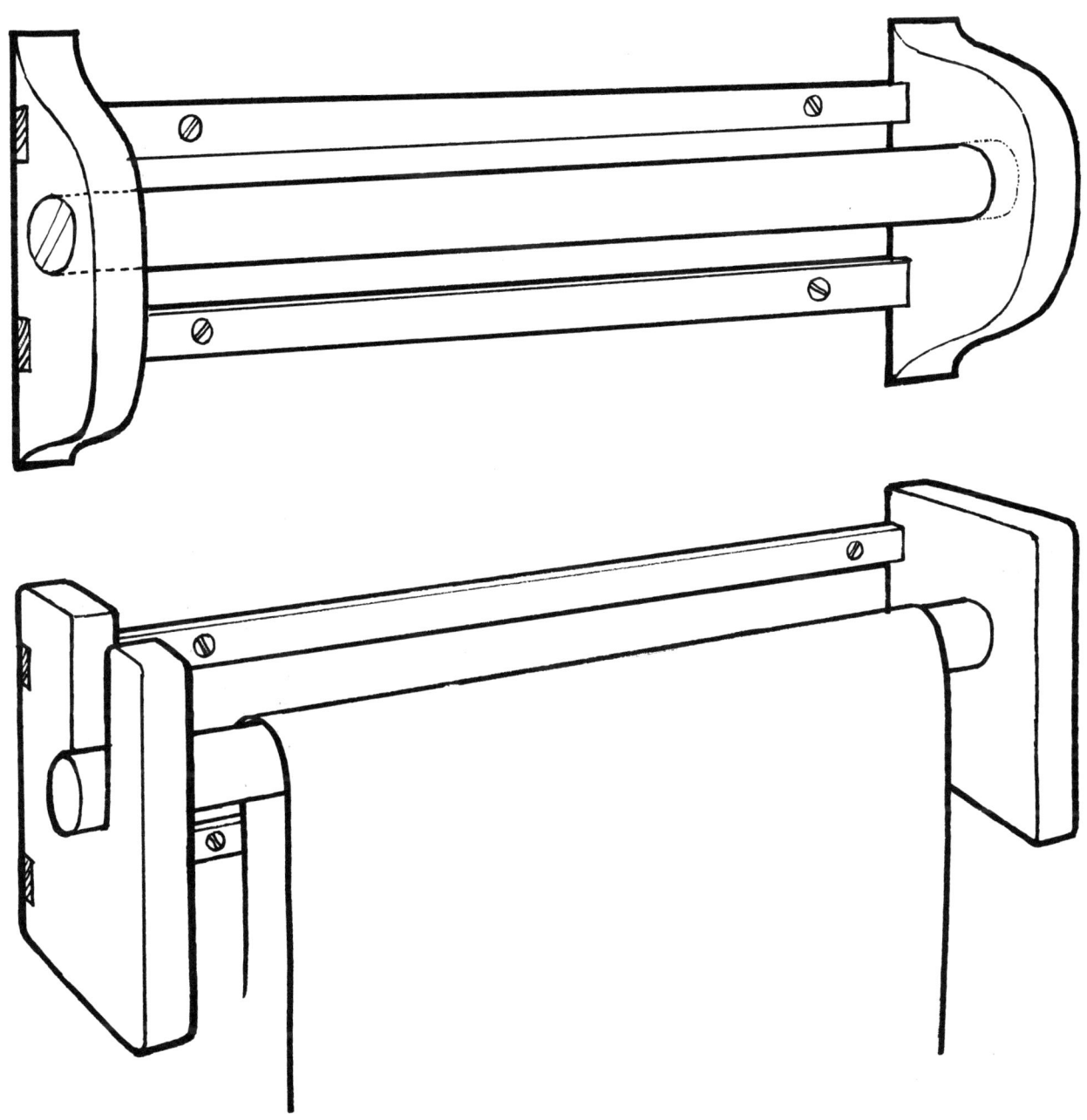

86
Trays

These seem to be made mainly for mom's birthday or just before Christmas and are always useful items. Copper corner pieces make a tray look nice and stronger to boot.

Materials: softwood or hardwood, surround, plywood bottom.

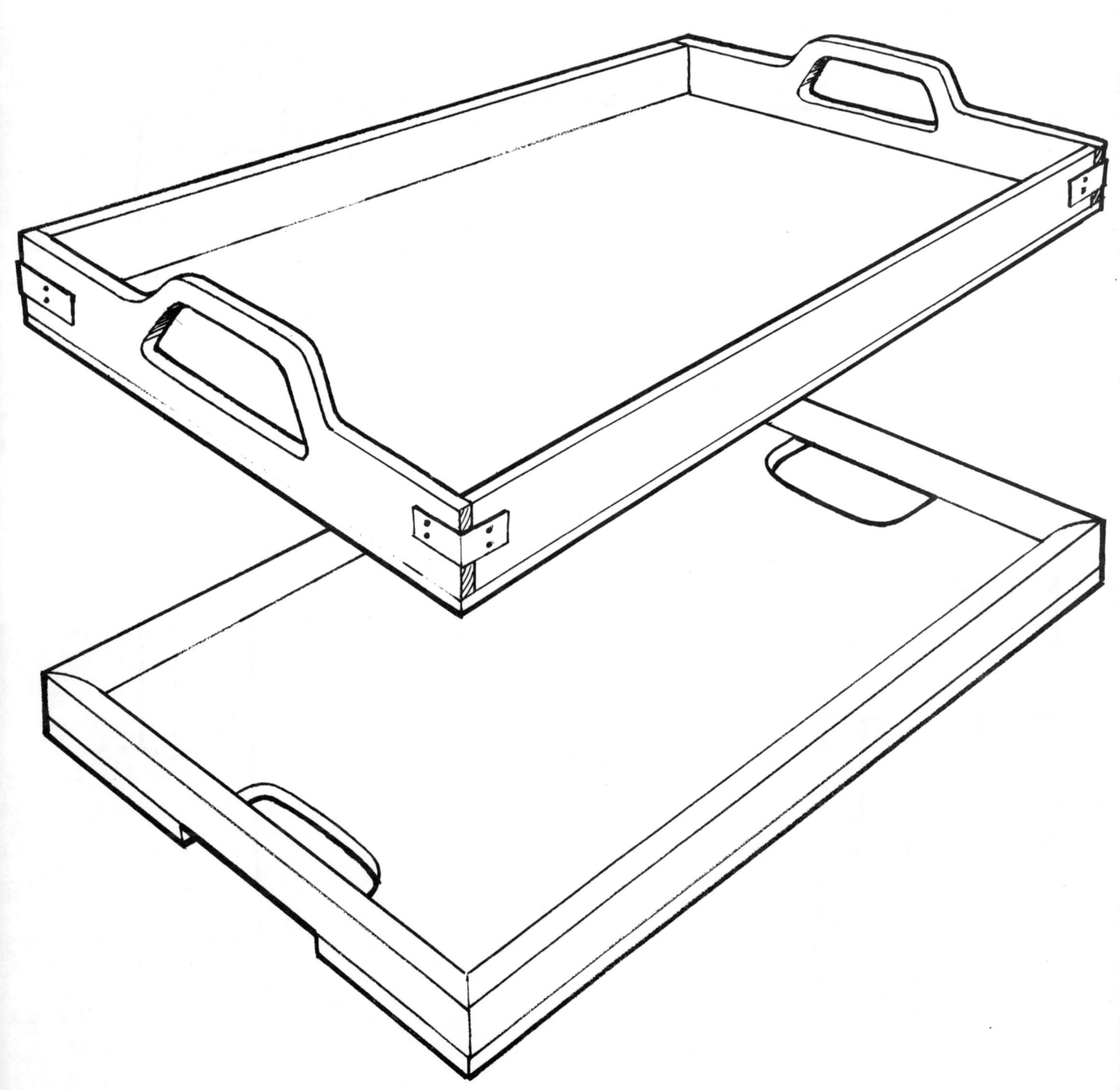

87
Birdhouses

The most natural type is the hollowed out log, but birds seem just as happy in a regular holed box. Provision must be made for removing the front so that the box can be cleaned out each year. Note that small birds will not nest if the hole is too large.

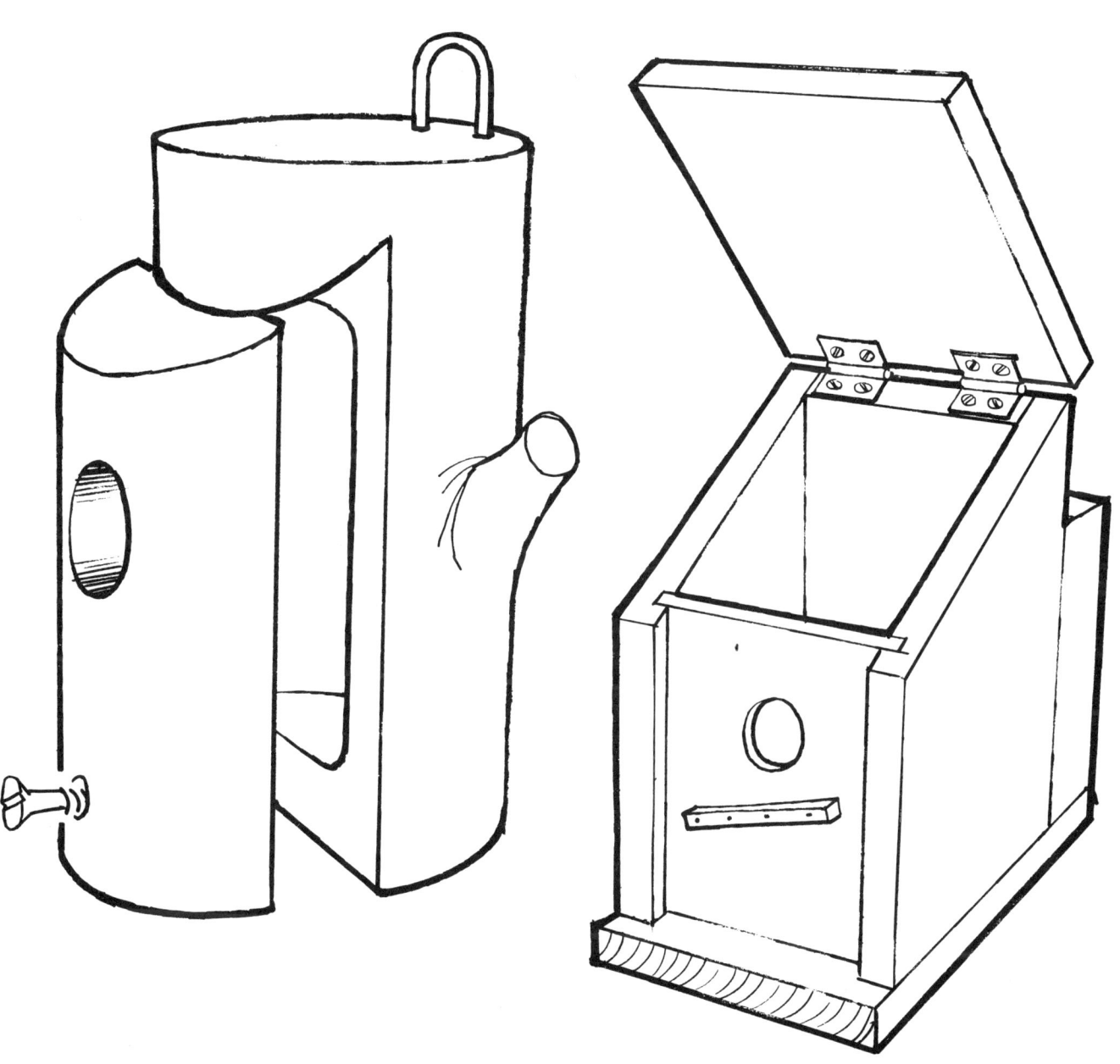

89
Solid Guitar Replica

These were made initially as stage props for an end-of-term play that the older boys were producing. They looked so impressive that other children made them as well for miming to rock records or simply to look good hanging on their walls.

Materials: chipboard, plywood, pine section, string, assorted knobs, paint.

90
Wooden Spoon

Each one different and individual. Cut out from a piece of hardwood and then hollowed out either by carving or using a wood bore in an electric drill.

   Materials: hardwood or softwood section.

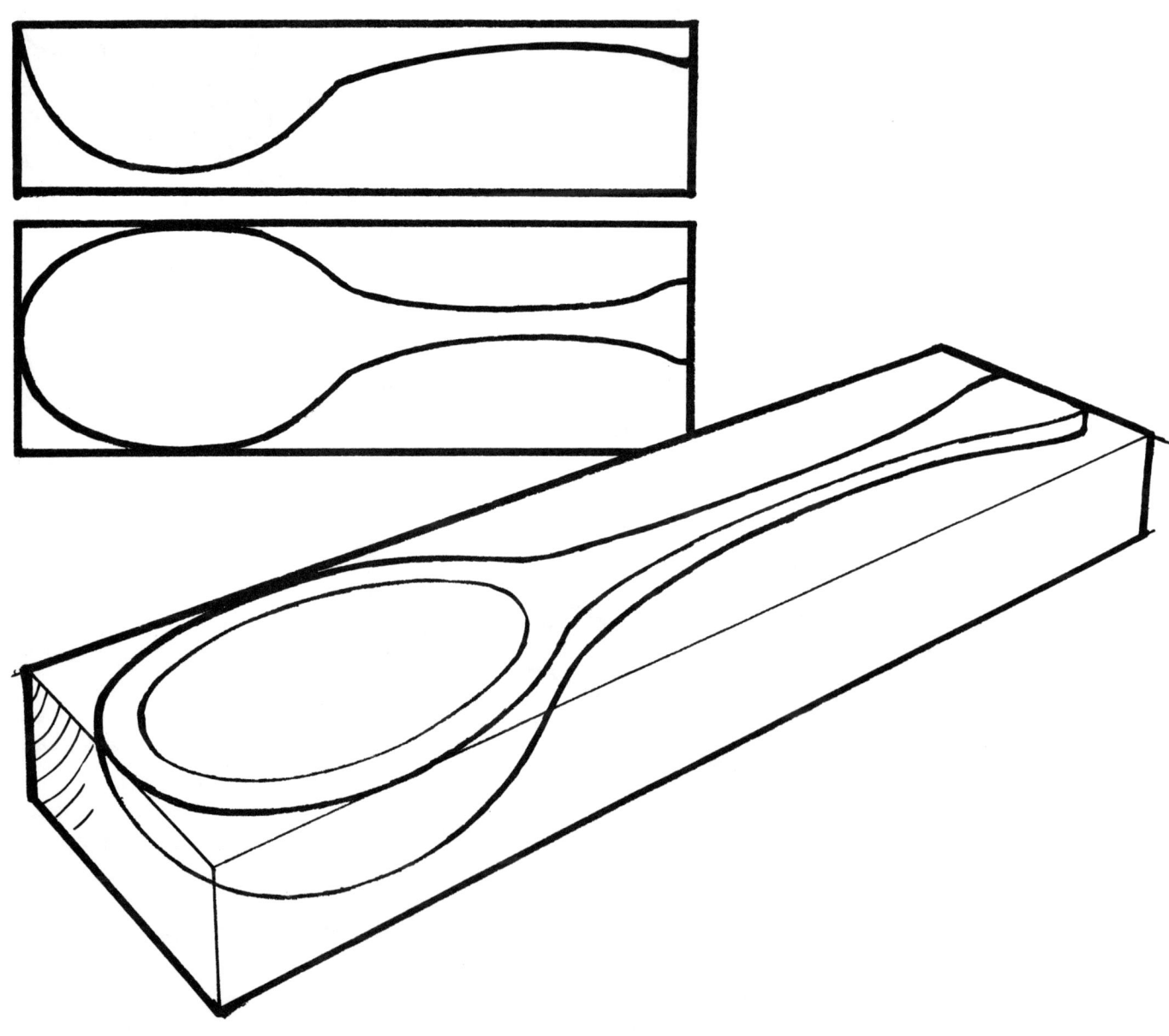

91
Plaster Eggs

These are just nice to have around. Mix up some plaster of paris so that it's fairly liquid (add color if required). Pour into a bottle. Then blow up a balloon and place the end of the balloon over the bottle neck. Pour in the plaster and swirl around until set. The balloon usually bursts due to heat generated by the setting plaster. Happy Easter.

92
Pull-Along Animal

These are simple animal cut-outs glued and nailed onto a board with wheels. They seem to be made mainly for younger brothers and sisters and look nice varnished or painted.

Materials: pine board or plywood.

93
Chopping Board

An absolute must in the kitchen. Small blocks or cubes of wood are glued together so that the end grain is uppermost. A frame strengthens the whole and finishes it off nicely. Make sure that the wood used for the blocks is well-seasoned, as any wood movement will cause cracks.

Materials: hardwood or softwood sections, vegetable oil for finish.

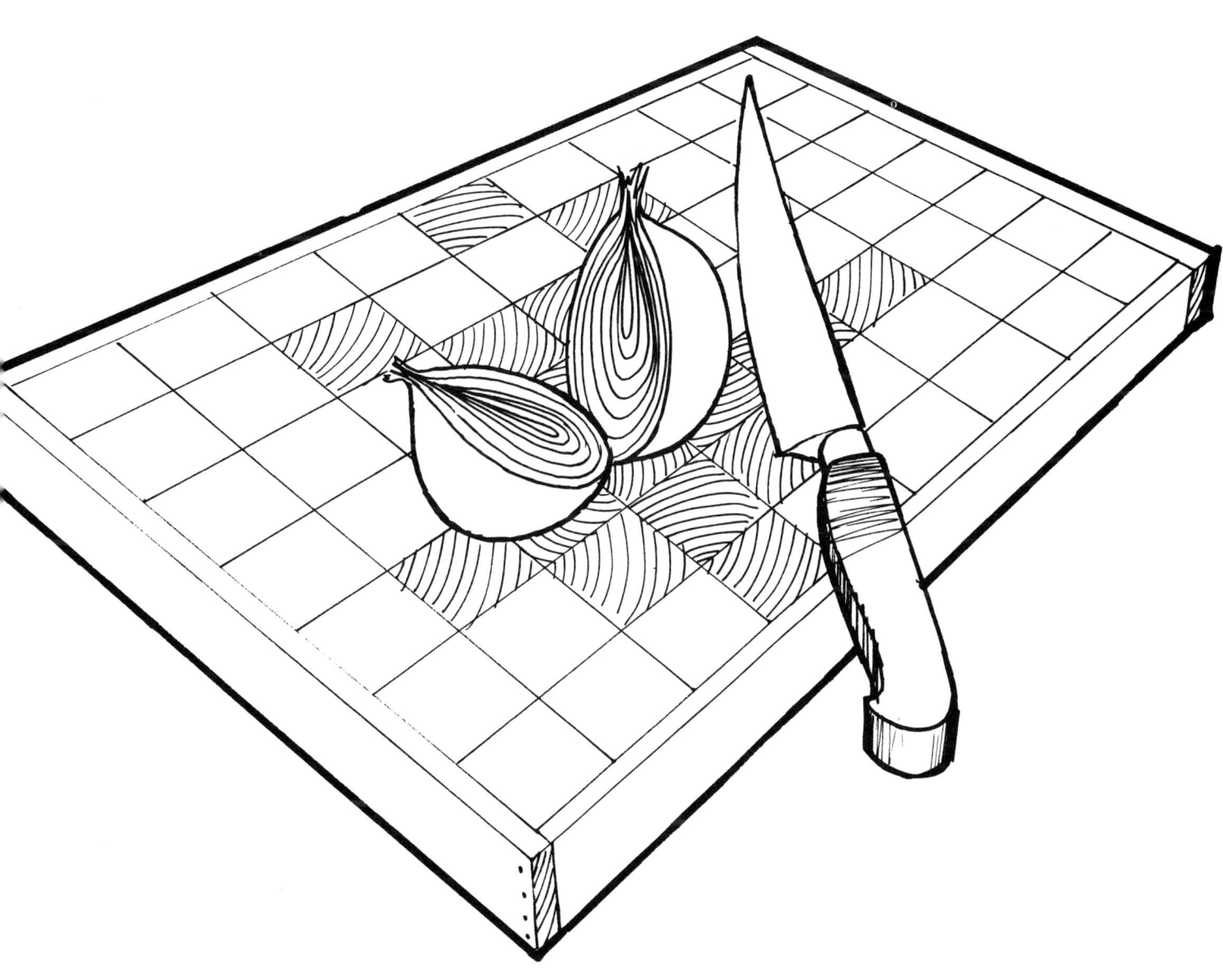

94
Sundry Boxes

Boxes of every size and shape for that special purpose, be it for tape cassettes or letter-writing materials. I made a special type box for a whole Brie cheese that I was giving as a present.

Materials: box catches, thin pine or hardwood board.

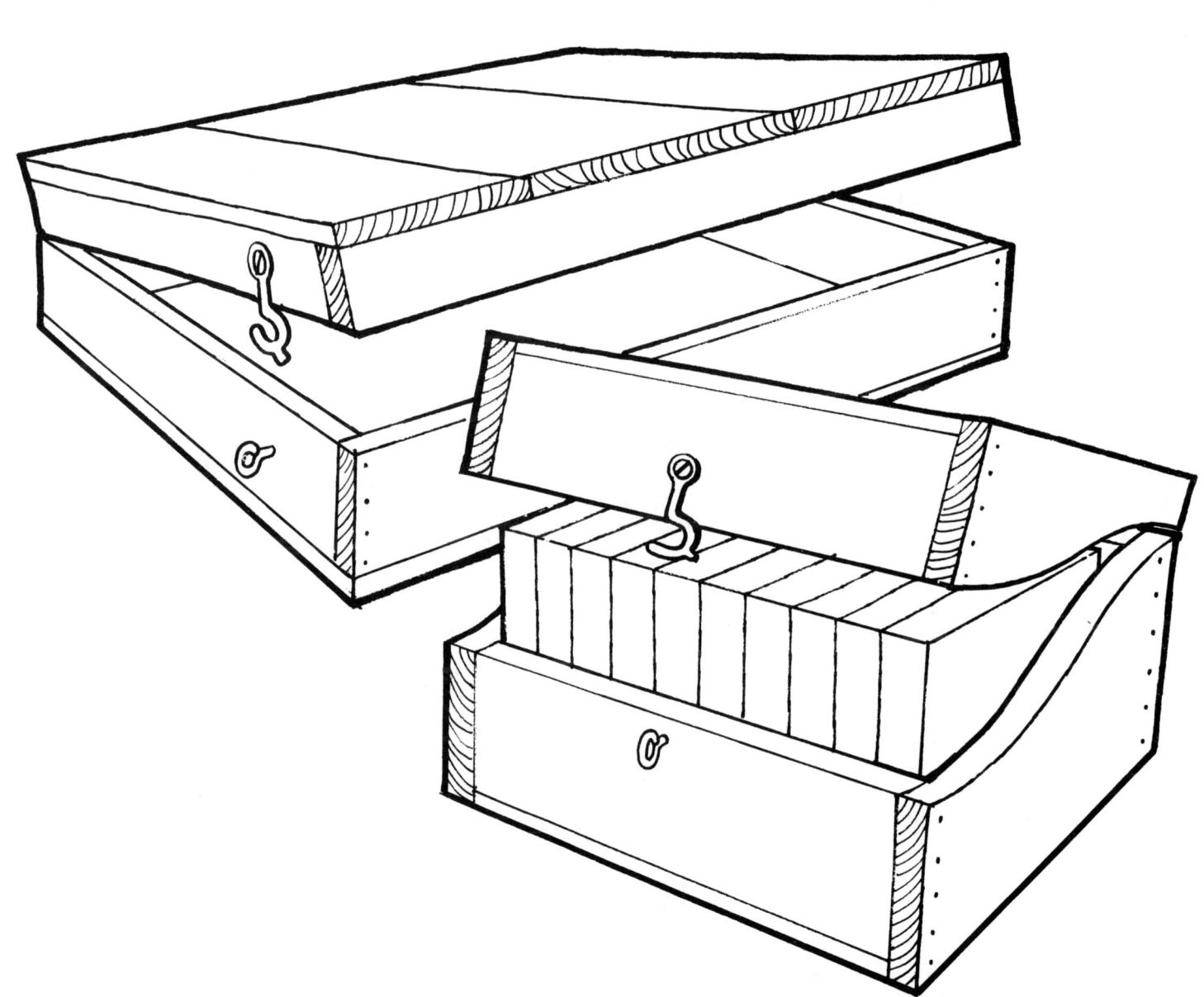

95
Boot Pull

The boot pull is a sloping board with a wedge cut out for the heel to fit into. One foot holds the board down while the other boot is removed. An absolute must in country areas.

Materials: pine board and section.

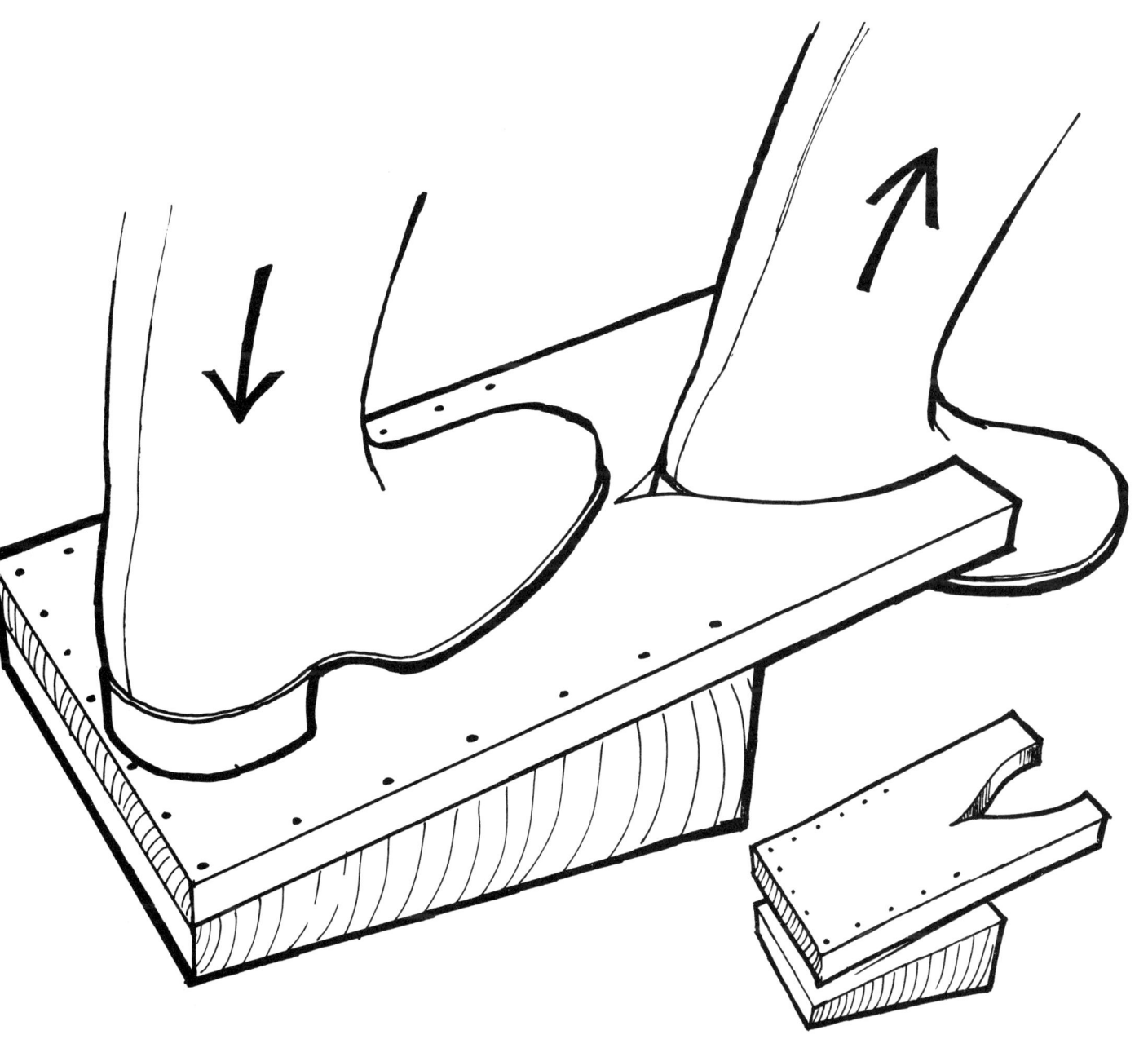

96
Signs

Make a sign and paint or brand a message.
　Materials: pine board or plywood.

98
Sundial

This tends to be made during the summer. Calibrate time against shadow using your watch. Then the next day check your watch against sundial time.

Materials: six-inch nail, pine board.

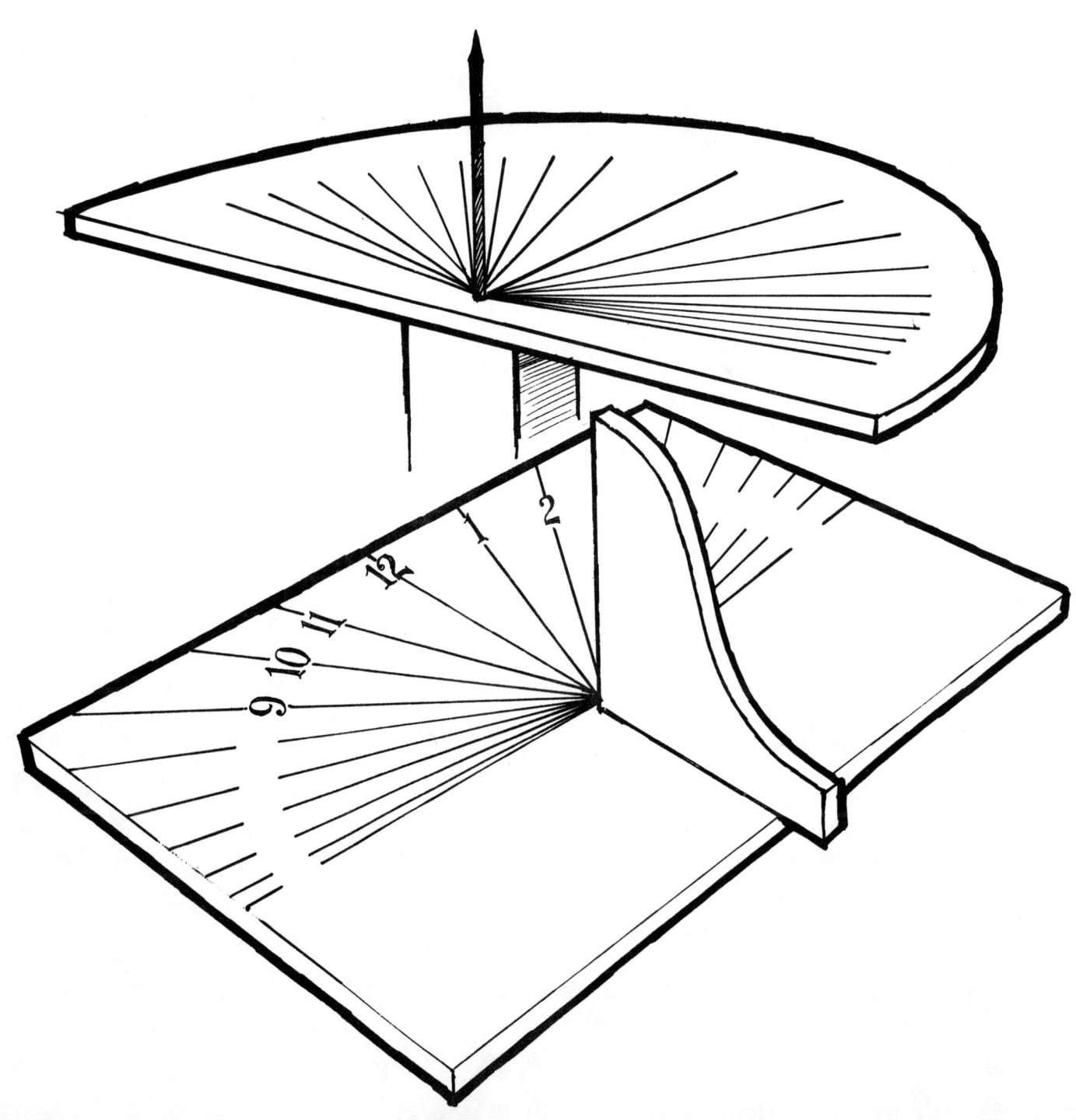

99
Roll Blinds

Simple and very attractive. The canvas can be dyed and decorated in many ways: batik, screen print, or paint on dyes. The blind poles simply hook onto a pair of double coat hooks. A reasonable finish for the canvas is a coating of paraffin wax ironed into the fabric.

Materials: canvas, poles, dyes, paraffin wax, coat hooks.

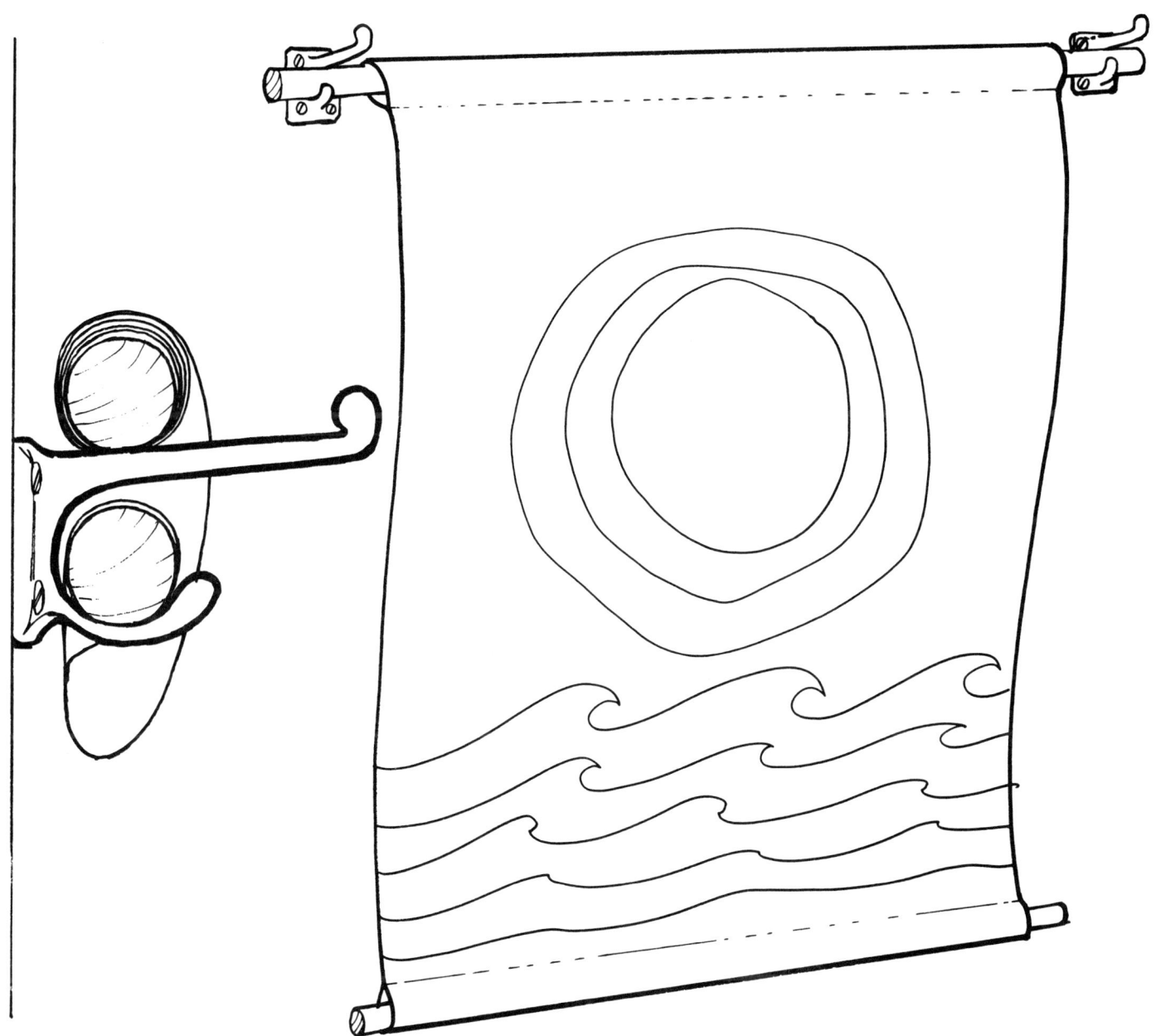

100
Clothespin Mat

Split the clothespins into their two wooden parts and arrange in a round or oval shape.
Materials: large supply of clothespins and heat resistant glue.

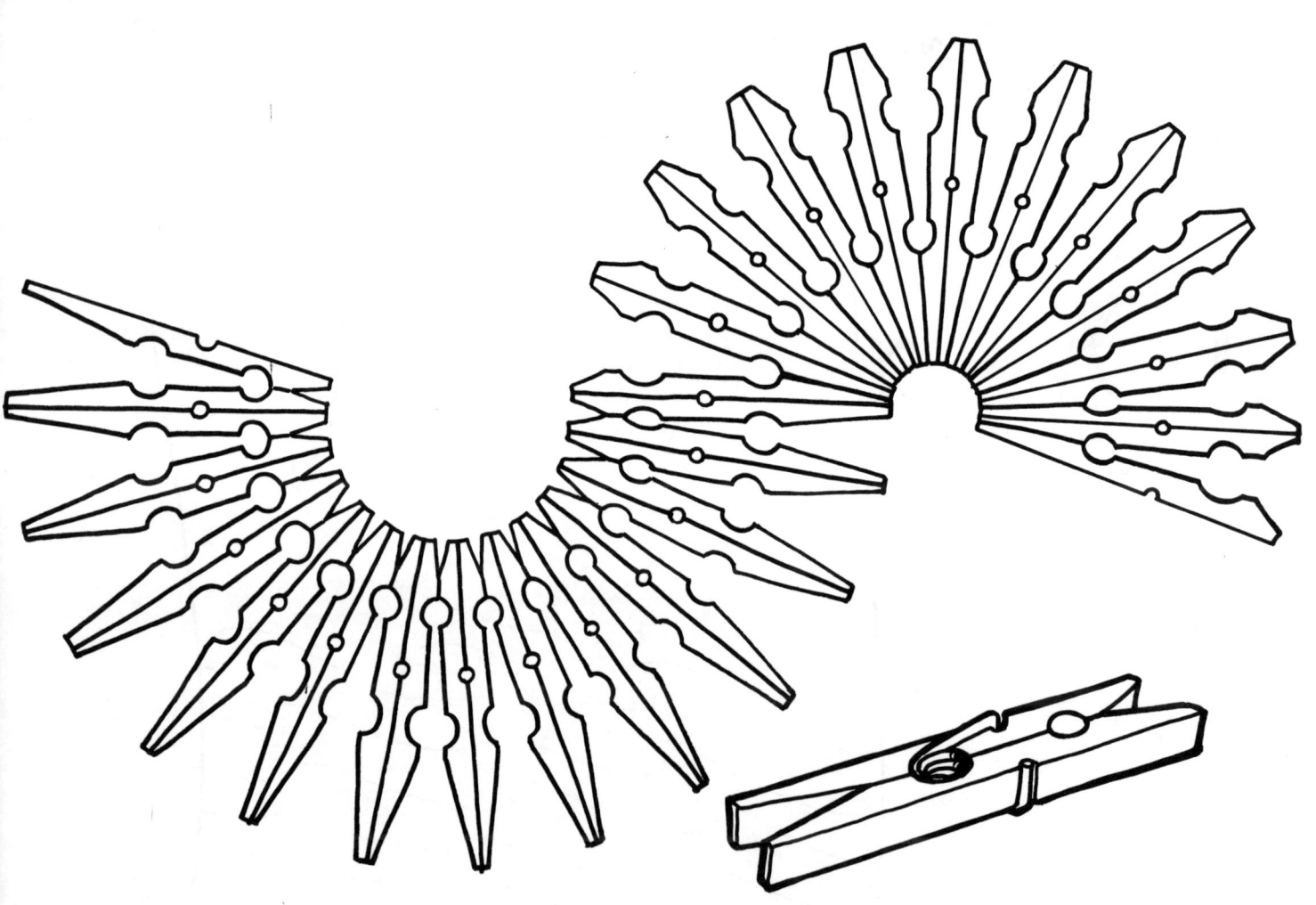

101
Glass Pictures

Off-cuts of glass can be engraved with a glass cutter to make a picture or pattern. Ink or shoe polish rubbed into the cuts makes the image clearer. Easily framed as well.

Materials: glass and wood section.

102
Trash Can Decoration

Any clean large can or container can be painted outside and magazine cut-outs pasted on for decoration.

103
Storage Jar Decoration

Jars used for storing dry goods, like rice, can be decorated inside or outside by sticking on cut-outs. A padded stick is essential for working on the inside of jars.

104
Mirror Picture

When a mirror breaks don't throw it away. Using tile cement carefully glue the pieces (spaced out) onto a board and fill the gaps with a plaster or putty. Makes a really interesting wall plaque.
Materials: mirror pieces, board, tile cement, putty, pinewood section.

NOTES